Fun
with
Stitching

Fun

with

Stitching

**35 cute sewing projects to turn
everyday items into works of art**

Fiona Goble

First published in 2011 by
New Holland Publishers (UK) Ltd
London Cape Town Sydney Auckland

Garfield House, 86–88 Edgware Road,
London W2 2EA, United Kingdom

www.newhollandpublishers.com

80 McKenzie Street, Cape Town 8001, South Africa
Unit 1, 66 Gibbes Street, Chatswood, NSW 2067, Australia
218 Lake Road, Northcote, Auckland, New Zealand

ISBN 978 1 84773 752 6

Senior Editor: Lisa John
Photography: Mark Winwood
Production: Laurence Poos
Design: Paul Stradling
Illustrations: Kuo Kang Chen
Publisher: Clare Sayer

2 4 6 8 10 9 7 5 3 1

Reproduction by Modern Age Repro House Ltd, Hong Kong
Printed and bound in Singapore by Tien Wah Press (PTE) Ltd

Some of the projects in this book are unsuitable for children under
3 years of age due to small parts. Always keep small or sharp
objects (such as needles or buttons) away from small children.

Contents

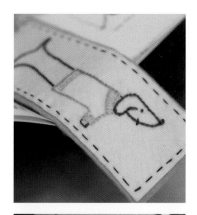

Introduction 6

The stitcher's kit 8

Stitching essentials 11

How to use the patterns 17

The projects

Eat 18

Sleep 32

Work 42

Relax 52

Play 62

Dress 72

Bath 84

Celebrate 94

Make your own stuff to stitch 104

The patterns 110

Index 127

Acknowledgements 128

Introduction

There is something of a buzz in the air about embroidery at the moment. I don't mean everyone's about to start stitching delicate flowers onto linen tablecloths all over again, but people are beginning to want clothes and home accessories that are a bit different. To my way of thinking, there's nothing easier and more enjoyable than customizing a few possessions with some carefully chosen stitches.

You probably know some of the basic stitches already. Even if you don't, I've explained them all here and I'm sure you'll be able to pick them up in no time. You can buy embroidery thread and needles in almost any sewing or craft shop and in some big department stores, and get going right away. You can transform something ordinary into something special really swiftly – sometimes in just a few minutes.

There are so many things that can be embellished by a bit of embroidery – some items you may already have and some you can make yourself. I've only used a small selection of handmade items here, and I've written some brief instructions on how to make them on pages 106–109.

But you don't have to stop with these. You can make and embroider spectacle cases, fabric photo frames, wash bags, table runners, peg bags... the possibilities are almost endless.

Sometimes embroidery is about trial and error. And sometimes it's just about what takes your fancy. So browse through the book and have a look through your home and wardrobe and decide where you want to start. Above all, I hope you have fun.

Fiona Goble

The stitcher's kit

One of the best things about the stitching bug is that you only need a few basic bits of equipment to get started. Better still, all the items are relatively inexpensive. If you don't already have these items in your sewing or craft box, you can easily get hold of these from most craft shops or from online craft or sewing stores.

The basics

Embroidery needle
Embroidery needles have sharp points and eyes that are big enough to thread six-strand embroidery thread. A medium-size embroidery needle is suitable for all the projects in this book.

Embroidery thread (floss)
I have sewn all the projects in this book with ordinary six-strand embroidery thread (floss) that comes in a rainbow of different colours. The colours you buy will depend on the projects you want to make but it's a good idea to start out by buying a selection of basic colours that you can then add to. Most embroidery threads sold in craft shops are colourfast but it is worth checking just to make sure. Even if you are embroidering something you don't plan to wash, you will probably still need to spray it with water to remove the marks from your water-soluble pen or quilter's pencil (see Methods of transfering your pattern, right).

For most of the projects in this book, you will need to use three strands of embroidery thread. In other words, you will need to cut a length of six-strand thread then divide it in two. In some cases you will need to use fewer or more strands of thread.

Embroidery thread comes in little skeins that are kept together with one or two paper loops. These skeins can easily get tangled so you might want to take some steps to make sure your threads behave.

The easiest way to do this is to wind the whole skein of thread onto a special bobbin that you can buy in craft stores. Alternatively, you could wind the thread around a piece of card with a little slit along one side to hold the end of the thread in place.

Fabric
You can embroider almost any fabric. Good fabrics for beginners are medium-weight woven cottons, tightly woven linen and felt. Avoid fabrics that are very stiff, shaggy or very heavily textured. Also avoid fabrics with a very loose weave, since these could pucker easily and stitches such as French knots (see page 16) could slip through your work and spoil it.

You can embroider stretchy materials such as cotton T-shirts and fleece, although these aren't ideal for beginners because they need a little bit more care.

Methods of transferring your pattern
There are three main methods to transfer your pattern to your fabric:
• A water-soluble pen or quilter's pencil (these work like an ordinary felt tip or pencil but are easily removed with water);
• Dressmaker's carbon paper or transfer paper and an ordinary pencil;
• A special transfer pen or pencil, some tracing paper, an ordinary pencil and an iron.

For the first two methods you will also need access to a photocopier, a computer with a scanner, or some tracing paper and a black pen.

Each of the three pattern transfer methods will produce a clear outline for you to stitch. For more details about transferring your pattern, see page 17.

Embroidery scissors

These are small, sharp scissors and I strongly advise you to buy a pair if you do not already have some. Because they are small, they're easier to use than other scissors when snipping thread when you've finished stitching.

The small points are also useful if you need to undo any work. You can use them to pull the thread to undo a few stitches or to snip stitches before pulling them out.

Helpful extras

Trimmings

For some of the projects you will need trimmings such as buttons, braid or bias binding. It's a good idea to build up a selection of items like these so you have a choice. The type of trimmings you choose can make a big diference to the look of your project.

Standard sewing needle

You will need this sort of needle in order to sew any embellishments on to your embroidery, such as the buttons that feature in some of the projects.

Embroidery hoops

Embroidery hoops consist of two rings – a smaller fixed ring and an adjustable ring. The idea is that you stretch your fabric across the smaller ring then fit it inside the adjustable ring. Hoops are available in a range of sizes and in wood or plastic.

Many people find that hoops make embroidering much easier, but they are not essential, particularly when you are stitching quite sturdy fabrics. Also, you should not use a hoop when embroidering on felt as it will pull the fabric out of shape.

Thimble

If your fingers become sore from pushing the needle through your fabric, it is worth getting a thimble – though it can take a bit of getting used to.

Stabilizer fabrics

If your fabric is very flimsy or stretchy, you may want to add a stabilizer fabric to the back of it (although I find it perfectly easy to embroider T-shirts without a stabilizer if I stick to a small chain stitch). The most popular stabilizer fabric is an iron-on version that you can tear away from the back of your fabric once your stitching is complete. You can buy this in shops that sell embroidery and sewing supplies, and in online stores.

Iron

You don't have to iron your embroidery projects, particularly if you are embroidering felt or fleece, but an iron is useful for projects you've stitched on crisp cotton or linen. Always press your work on the back and be careful not to press your embroidery work too heavily as this will make the stitches look flat.

Sew your own

If you're planning to make your own items to embroider you will also need:

Sewing scissors

A good-quality pair of sewing scissors is essential for cutting fabric. Remember to keep them strictly for cutting fabric as they will quickly become blunt if you use them for cutting paper or card.

Pins

Sharp pins are essential for pinning most of the projects together before you sew. The ones with coloured glass heads are useful as they are less likely to get left in your work by mistake.

Sewing machine

This is optional as you can sew most of the items in the book by hand. However, a machine will make sewing-up much quicker and help give you professional-looking results.

Supply of fabrics

The exact fabrics you need depend on what you are making, but a collection of neutral or pastel cottons and linens is a great starting point. Some floral fabrics that you can use to make your own binding will also come in useful (see pages 105 and 108). Remember to pre-shrink your fabrics by washing them before you unleash your creative talent. Once your work is complete, wash the items by hand in cool water only, just to be on the safe side.

Stitching essentials

There are loads of embroidery stitches, but all the stitches and techniques you need for the projects in this book are listed below.

Starting and finishing your work

The easiest way to secure your work at the beginning is simply to tie a knot at the end of your embroidery thread that is large enough not to slip through your fabric. If you prefer not to have knots on the back of your work or are embroidering a particularly fine fabric and using small stitches, leave a 4-cm (1½-in) 'tail' of thread at the back of your work and simply start stitching. Once you have finished your work you can weave the tail through the back of your stitches.

Once you've finished, the easiest way to secure your work is to sew a knot at the back.

To do this, take your thread to the back of your work. Pass your needle under the last stitch, then through the loop you have just made. Tighten the knot and snip your thread close to the knot. If you prefer not to have a knot and are using small stitches, you can simply weave the thread through the stitches then snip it off.

Stitch library

All the stitches used within this book are explained and illustrated over the next few pages. Most of the stitches are extremely easy and you may be familiar with them already.

Straight stitch
A straight stitch is just a simple single stitch or group of single stitches, like the stitches used to make up a running stitch.

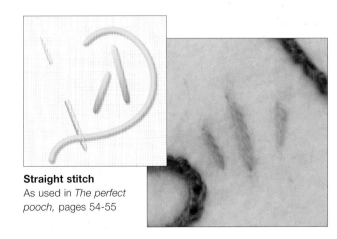

Straight stitch
As used in *The perfect pooch,* pages 54-55

Star stitch

A star stitch is really a group of straight stitches that are worked across each other to form a star shape.

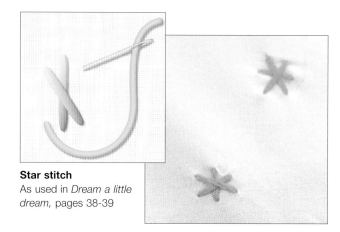

Star stitch
As used in *Dream a little dream*, pages 38-39

Running stitch

For running stitch, simply insert your needle and take it a stitch width along your fabric and back out again. You can work several running stitches at a time. Running stitch can be worked in different lengths and with different size spaces – but always keep your stitch length and spacing even.

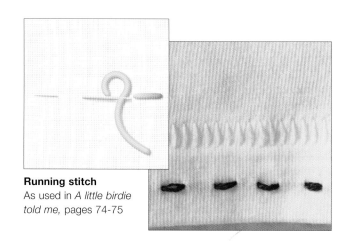

Running stitch
As used in *A little birdie told me,* pages 74-75

Threaded running stitch

Threaded running stitch is simply a strand of coloured thread sewn along a row of running stitches. Start your second thread at the same point as your running stitches. Simply weave down under the thread of the first running stitch and up under the thread of the second running stitch, without stitching through the fabric. Continue weaving up and down until you come to the end of the running stitches.

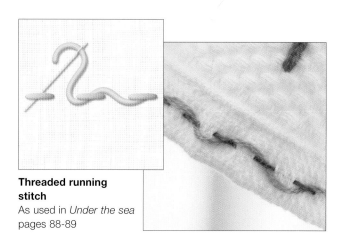

Threaded running stitch
As used in *Under the sea* pages 88-89

Back stitch

To start, make one forward stitch as if you were working a simple running stitch and bring your needle out to the front of your fabric, a stitch width to the left (1). Then take the needle back into your fabric at the ending point of the stitch you have just made (2) then up through the fabric at 3, a stitch width to the left of the new stitch.

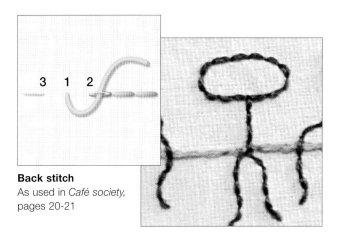

Back stitch
As used in *Café society*, pages 20-21

Stem stitch

Starting at point 1, take your needle to point 2 and then backwards to point 3, which is about half way between the other two points. You can sew round curves using stem stitch but you might need to make your stitches slightly smaller when you do this to make sure the finished curve looks smooth.

When you are using stem stitch, it is important to always keep your thread on the same side of your needle. If you are sewing a straight line, it doesn't matter which side this is. If you are sewing a curve, keep the thread to the inside of the curve.

To keep your threads neat when working stem stitch around a corner, take your needle to the back of your work at the corner and tie a knot, as explained in *Starting and finishing your work* on page 11 – but do not trim your thread. Instead, take your needle back out to the front to continue stitching.

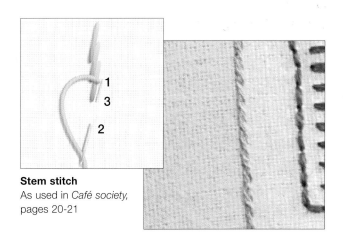

Stem stitch
As used in *Café society*, pages 20-21

Satin stitch

This stitch is used to 'fill in' an area with colour with a series of straight lines, as with the boy's cheeks in the example shown. Take your needle out of your work at 1, back down at 2, out again at 3, down again at 4, out again at 5 and continue in this way until the shape you want to fill is complete. If your shape does not turn out as perfectly even along the sides as you would like, you can work round the sides using a small back stitch.

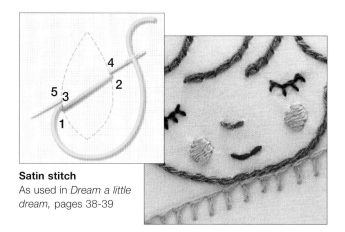

Satin stitch
As used in *Dream a little dream,* pages 38-39

Chain stitch

Take your needle out at the starting point for your stitch (1). Now take your needle back into your fabric, just next to your starting point (2), remembering not to pull the thread too tightly so there is a little loop of thread. Then bring your needle back up through your fabric a stitch width along (3) and catch in the loop. Pull your thread up so it is firm but not too tight.

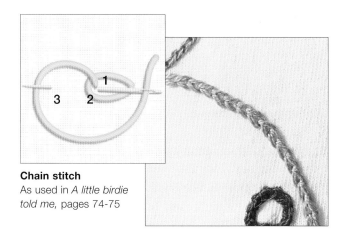

Chain stitch
As used in *A little birdie told me,* pages 74-75

Lazy daisy stitch

The lazy daisy stitch is really a group of single chain stitches, all starting around a single point. To make the first stitch, make a single chain stitch as described above. Secure the loop to the fabric with a small stitch then take your needle to the starting point of the next stitch.

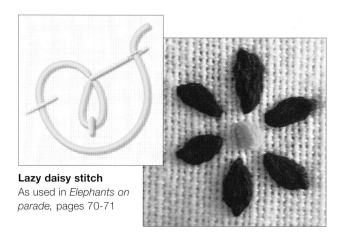

Lazy daisy stitch
As used in *Elephants on parade,* pages 70-71

Scallop stitch

This stitch is a bit like working a lazy daisy stitch where the beginning and end of the chain stitch are not so close together. Scallop stitches are usually worked as a series. You can make the stitches fairly wide or much narrower, as shown here. From your starting point (1), take your needle down through your fabric (2) leaving a little loop of thread. Bring your needle out of your fabric again where you want your stitch to end (3) and pass your needle under the loop of thread. Pull your stitch fairly taut. Secure the loop by taking your needle down through your fabric, just to the outer side of the loop (4). Bring the needle out again at 2 to start the next stitch.

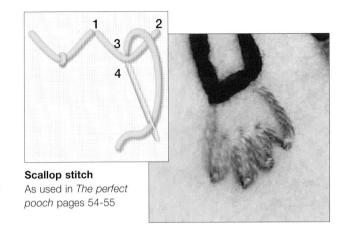

Scallop stitch
As used in *The perfect pooch* pages 54-55

Blanket stitch

Io start, take your needle out on the line or edge that you are embroidering (1). Take the needle down through your fabric a stitch length and a stitch width to the left (2). Bring your needle up on the line, immediately above where you have taken it down (3), making sure you have caught the thread under the needle tip. Pull the thread fairly tightly.

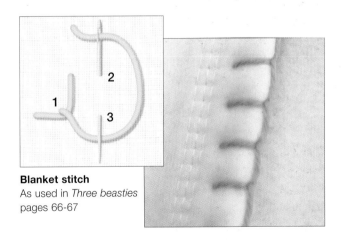

Blanket stitch
As used in *Three beasties* pages 66-67

French knot

To make a French knot, it's easier to work with a fairly short length of thread and to make the stitch close to your fabric. First, bring your thread up at your starting point and wind the thread twice around the needle (1). (Some of the projects in this book involve winding the thread around just once and if this is the case I'll mention it in the instructions.)

Holding the thread taut, take the tip of your needle back into your fabric, just to the side of your starting point (2). It is important you don't take your needle back into the exact starting point or your knot will slip through your fabric! Continue pulling your needle through your work and slide the knot off the needle and onto your fabric. Either tie a knot beneath the fabric to hold the French knot in place or take it back to the front ready to work the next stitch.

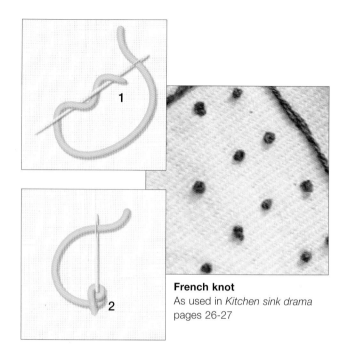

French knot
As used in *Kitchen sink drama* pages 26-27

Sorting out tangles and knots

Sometimes when you're stitching, your thread may appear to have developed a knot. This is usually because the thread has become twisted and you can undo it by pulling the thread gently on either side of the 'knot'.

At other times the strands of the floss might look a bit uneven or tangled. To sort this out, run your fingers along the length of the thread to smooth it out.

Knot-free stitching ahoy *Sail away with me* pages 92-93

How to use the patterns

There are a number of ways to transfer the patterns in this book onto your fabric. The method you choose is partly down to your own preference. It will also depend on the type of fabric you are using and whether you are embroidering a simple piece of fabric or a ready-made item.

Remember that the patterns are all shown at the actual size they have been used in the projects photographed. You can make the patterns smaller or larger to suit your particular project, either on a photocopier or by scanning it into a computer. But remember, some patterns might not work as well if they are made very big and if you make them too small, some of the patterns will be tricky to stitch.

Method 1

Tracing directly onto your fabric

If you are using a fairly thin fabric, you can trace the design directly onto the fabric.

You will need access to a photocopier, or a computer with a scanner or some tracing paper and a black pen. You will also need a water-soluble pen or quilter's pencil.

Either photocopy, scan and print or trace the pattern. Then tape the pattern onto a sunny window and trace it directly on to your fabric using a water-soluble pen or quilter's pencil.

If you own a light box (a box with a light inside and a translucent white glass or plastic cover) or are prepared to invest in one, this will save you relying on the weather or time of day!

Method 2

Using dressmaker's carbon paper or transfer paper

You can use this method to transfer your design onto any weight of fabric.

You will need access to a photocopier, or a computer with a scanner or some tracing paper and a black pen. You will also need a piece of dressmaker's carbon paper or transfer paper, in a colour that will show up on your fabric, and an ordinary pencil.

Either photocopy, scan and print or trace the pattern. Lay the carbon or transfer paper face down on your fabric. Then place the pattern on top of the paper and trace round it with a pencil. When you lift the carbon or transfer paper away, the design will have been transferred to the fabric.

Method 3

Using a transfer pen or pencil

First trace the image on to tracing paper using an ordinary pencil. Then turn the paper over and trace over the lines your have already made using a transfer pen or pencil. Tape the paper, transfer side down, and transfer with an iron, following the instructions that come with the transfer pen or pencil.

> **Note**
> *All the measurements in this book are given in metric units (millimetres or centimetres) with the imperial units (inches or fractions of an inch) given in brackets afterwards, usually to the nearest ¼ in. Because it is difficult to convert small units of measurement exactly, it is important that you use one system or the other rather than a mix of the two.*

Eat

Café society

Who can resist popping in for coffee at a traditional street café in Paris? The smell of freshly-made coffee, the delicious pastries, the dapper waiters – and even the cheesy accordion music. Now you can create your own French café anywhere you like. I made this apron using a vintage apron pattern but you could easily use a ready-made apron or a modern pattern. Surf the web for some ideas and free patterns.

Get stitching ...

First transfer the café pattern on page 110 onto your apron pocket or pocket fabric.

Work around the top and sides of the roof canopy in chain stitch using three strands of bright red embroidery thread. With the same thread, work the stripes and lower edge in back stitch and a row of scallop stitches along the lower edge.

Work around the plant in chain stitch using three strands of leaf green embroidery thread. Work the stem and branches in back stitch using three strands of dark brown embroidery thread. Work the plant pot in chain stitch using three strands of terracotta embroidery thread.

Work the outline of the building in stem stitch using three strands of caramel embroidery thread.

Work the table and chairs in back stitch using three strands of dark grey embroidery thread.

Work the café door in stem stitch using three strands of mint green embroidery thread. Using the same thread, work the door panels in running stitch. Use the same thread again for the two lazy daisy stitches and French knot. Work a single French knot for the doorknob using six strands of dark grey embroidery thread.

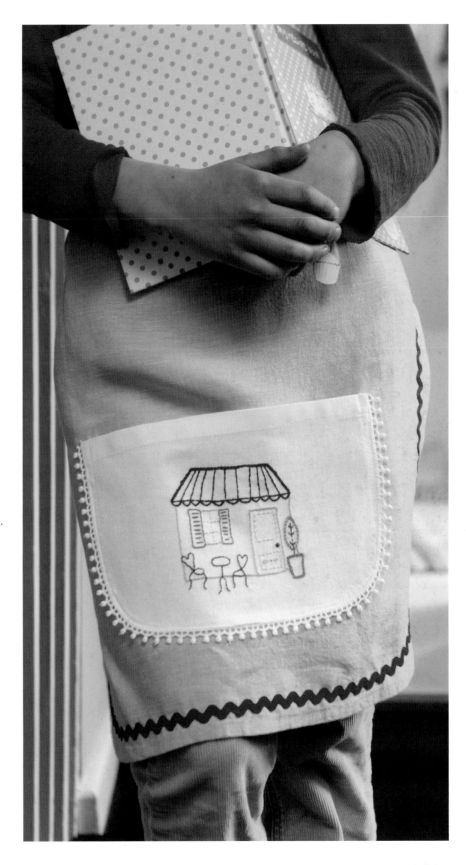

 Work the table and chairs in back stitch, using three strands of dark grey embroidery thread.

 Work the shutters in back stitch and the shutter louvres in straight stitch using three strands of royal blue embroidery thread. Work the top and bottom of the window in back stitch using three strands of pale grey embroidery thread. Work the windowpanes in running stitch using the same thread.

 Before stitching the pocket in place, I rounded the lower corners, made a double hem at the top and pressed under the raw edges. I also added some white lace around the edge.

stitch it!

This design would also look great on a plain tea towel, as a small picture for a kitchen or dining room or on a cushion with a lace border.

A nice cup of tea

Whatever the weather and whatever the time of day, there's nothing more refreshing than a nice cup of tea. And it has to be in one of my favourite spotty cups, immortalized here. I made the tablemats from scraps of fabric in my stash. You could easily buy fabric mats to embroider but if you want to make your own, turn to page 104.

Get stitching ...

First transfer the teacup and saucer pattern on page 110 onto the centre of your tablemat. If you are making your own mats, transfer the pattern onto the centre of the central fabric panel before you sew the mat pieces together.

Work the outline of the main part of the cup and saucer in chain stitch using three strands of royal blue or red embroidery thread. Using the same thread, work the handle in stem stitch and the inner ring of the saucer in running stitch.

Work the spots in chain stitch using three strands of pale blue embroidery thread on the royal blue cup and three strands of lime green embroidery thread on the red cup.

If you are making your own mats, now sew the mat pieces together.

stitch it!

This design would also look great on the corner of large linen napkins, on a striped tea towel or on a greeting card for a friend.

Let them eat cake

When you need a little afternoon pick-me-up, nothing fits the bill quite so well as a delicious cupcake. The sensation of sinking your teeth through the swirl of icing and soft sponge is hard to beat. So why not embroider these napkins to accompany your teatime treat? I used large linen napkins for this project and dyed them pink. If you want to make your own napkins, simply double hem a 50-cm (20-in) square of linen or cotton fabric.

Get stitching ...

First transfer the cake pattern on page 111 onto the corner of your napkin.

Work the icing on top of the cupcakes in chain stitch using three strands of bright pink or bright yellow embroidery thread.

Work the sponge tops of the cupcake in stem stitch using three strands of pale beige embroidery thread.

Work the outline of the cupcake cases in chain stitch using three strands of lime green or turquoise embroidery thread. Work the vertical lines on the cases in back stitch using the same thread.

Work a line of large running stitches around the border of the napkins using three strands of deep yellow or red embroidery thread.

Sew the buttons in place on top of the icing, as shown in the picture.

You will need

- ✕ Embroidery thread (floss) in the following colours:
  Turquoise and lime green for the cupcake cases
  Pale beige for the sponge tops
  Bright yellow and bright pink for the icing
  Red and deep yellow for the napkin borders
- ✕ Embroidery needle
- ✕ Embroidery scissors
- ✕ Ready-made or handmade napkins
- ✕ Red button and green button for the cake decorations
- ✕ Sewing needle and thread to sew on the buttons

Stitches used

Running stitch, back stitch, stem stitch, chain stitch

stitch it!

This design would look great on a greeting card, a table runner, or a fabric doorstop for the kitchen.

Kitchen sink drama

Sometimes you've just got to embrace those domestic chores that could easily get you down – so add a bit of cheer to your kitchen towels with these brightly embroidered cooking utensils. Plain or simple striped tea towels work best for this project.

You will need

- ✕ Embroidery thread (floss) in the following colours:
  Turquoise for the whisk handle
  Dark grey for the whisk
  Crimson for the slotted spoon handle
  Purple for the slotted spoon
  Leaf green for the serving fork
- ✕ Embroidery needle
- ✕ Embroidery scissors
- ✕ Tea towel

Stitches used

Running stitch, back stitch, stem stitch, French knot

Get stitching ...

First transfer the kitchen utensils pattern on page 111 onto the corner of your tea towel.

Work the whisk handle in stem stitch using three strands of turquoise embroidery thread. Work the whisk in running stitch using three strands of dark grey embroidery thread.

Work the handle of the slotted spoon in stem stitch using three strands of crimson embroidery thread. Work the hole in the handle in back stitch using the same thread. Work the outline of the slotted spoon in stem stitch using three strands of purple embroidery thread. Using the same thread, work French knots to represent the spoon holes.

Work the outline of the serving fork in back stitch using three strands of leaf green embroidery thread. Using the same thread, work the hole in back stitch.

stitch it!
This motif would also look great on a fabric serving mat, a curtain for a kitchen, or an apron.

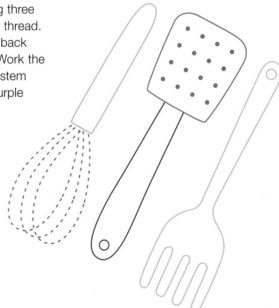

Sweetest little baby face

What self-respecting little angel wants a dreary plain bib when she could cheer up mealtimes in a bib like this? It's never too early to make your mark in the world of fashion. I used a ready-made bib but you could easily make your own. Surf the web for a pattern to download or make your own pattern from an existing bib.

Get stitching ...

First transfer the baby pattern on page 112 onto your bib.

Work around the outline of the baby's face in stem stitch using three strands of flesh-coloured embroidery thread. Using the same thread, work three tiny back stitches for the nose. Again using the same thread, work around the baby's hands in back stitch.

Work around the top in stem stitch, using three strands of turquoise embroidery thread.

Work around the hair in back stitch, using three strands of ginger brown embroidery thread.

Work French knots for the eyes using three strands of dark grey embroidery thread. Make three straight stitches using two strands of the same thread for the eyelashes.

Work the mouth in back stitch using three strands of red embroidery thread.

Embroider the cheeks in satin stitch using three strands of pale pink embroidery thread. If you need to neaten the edges of the satin stitch, work a ring of small back stitches.

Work around the spoon in back stitch using three strands of red embroidery thread. Then work tiny running stitches around the centre of the spoon.

Working in back stitch with three strands of embroidery thread, complete the bowl in lime green, the bottle top in purple and the bottle itself in royal blue. Using the same thread, add a few small straight stitches to the side of the bottle to indicate the measuring lines.

Work the table top in chain stitch using three strands of purple embroidery thread.

Sew the little bow just below the neckline of the baby's top.

You will need

✕ Embroidery thread (floss) in the following colours:
Flesh pink for the baby's head, nose and hands
Pale pink for the cheeks
Ginger brown for the hair
Turquoise for the baby's top
Purple for the table and bottle top
Royal blue for the bottle
Lime green for the bowl
Red for the mouth and spoon
Dark grey for the eyes and eyelashes

✕ Sewing needle

✕ Embroidery needle

✕ Embroidery scissors

✕ Woven cotton baby bib

✕ Small ready-made bow in pale turquoise – or a small length of narrow ribbon to make a bow yourself – and some matching thread to sew it on

Stitches used

Straight stitch, running stitch, back stitch, stem stitch, satin stitch, chain stitch, French knot

stitch it!
This motif would look great on a card to celebrate the birth of a baby, on a fabric cover for a photo album or on a baby's T-shirt.

Do the funky chicken

You will need

- ✗ Embroidery thread (floss) in the following colours:
  Purple for the chicken outline, wing and tail
  Orange for the legs and beak
  Dark grey for the eye
  Turquoise for the eye surround
  Bright pink for the breast
  Leaf green for the grass
  Crimson for the running stitch border
- ✗ Embroidery needle
- ✗ Embroidery scissors
- ✗ 22–23-cm (8¾–9-in) square of felt to make the cosy
- ✗ A water-soluble pen or quilter's pencil
- ✗ Fabric glue or standard sewing needle and thread to match your felt
- ✗ Sewing scissors

Stitches used

Straight stitch, running stitch, back stitch, stem stitch, lazy daisy stitch, French knot

stitch it!

This motif is also great on a simple felt egg cosy, a fabric pot holder or a set of Easter tablemats.

Chickens have always been popular in the kitchen. Chicken lovers can buy chicken-shaped chopping boards, kitchen timers, cookie cutters... you name it. So why not create your own chicken cup cosy to keep your coffee piping hot?

Get stitching...

First cut your cosy shape from the felt. Wrap the piece of felt around the cup. With a water-soluble pen or quilter's pencil, draw a line towards the top of the felt and a lower line, so the two lines are about 7 cm (2¾ in) apart. Cut along these lines. Finally, trim the side edges of the cosy so they are vertical and overlap by about 1 cm (⅜ in) at the back of the cup.

Transfer the pattern on page 112 onto the centre of the cosy.

Work the chicken outline in stem stitch using three strands of purple embroidery thread. Using the same thread, work the wing in back stitch. Work three lazy daisy stitches for the tail, again using the same thread.

Work the breast in small running stitches using three strands of bright pink embroidery thread.

Work a French knot for the eye using three strands of dark grey embroidery thread. Work straight stitches around the eye using two strands of turquoise embroidery thread.

Work the legs in back stitch using three strands of orange embroidery thread. Add the feet in straight stitch.

Work two straight stitches for the beak using six strands of orange embroidery thread.

Work the grass in straight stitches using three strands of leaf green embroidery thread.

Add a running stitch border round the entire cosy using six strands of crimson embroidery thread. Fasten the cosy at the back by overlapping the side edges and stitching or glueing them together.

Sleep

The cat's whiskers

In my next life, I'm definitely coming back as a cat so I can stretch out in the sunshine, have someone to wait on me and generally laze about. What could be more perfect? These pyjamas were made from a pattern I downloaded cheaply from a website – but you could just as easily embroider a pair of ready-made pyjamas or other garment.

Get stitching ...

First transfer the cat pattern on page 113 onto the pocket of the pyjama top.

Work the entire outline of the cat in stem stitch using three strands of pale grey embroidery thread.

Work the cat's stripes in chain stitch using three strands of terracotta embroidery thread.

Work the eyes and whiskers in back stitch using two strands of dark grey embroidery thread.

Work the nose in satin stitch using three strands of dark grey embroidery thread, adding a vertical straight stitch at the base.

stitch it!

Try this design on a greeting card for a feline lover, on a fabric bag or on a sweet little cushion.

Give me the moonlight

stitch it!

This motif looks great on a fabric doorstop for your bedroom, as a simple framed picture or on a simple drawstring bag to hold jewellery or special treasures.

If you've lived with the minimalist look for too long and want to bring a bit of fun and romance into your bedroom, why not embroider your own moonlight lampshade? The embroidered moon and the bright braid round the edges are the perfect way to perk up an inexpensive bedside lamp.

Get stitching ...

First transfer the pattern on page 113 onto the centre of your ivory lampshade. Alternatively, you could transfer the pattern to a piece of plain ivory fabric, which you can then use to cover your lampshade. If your lampshade has a plastic backing, it is a good idea to prick it with your needle before you make your stitches, as this will make it much easier to stitch.

Work around the outline of the moon in chain stitch using three strands of deep yellow embroidery thread.

Work the nose, eyebrows and upper part of the eyes in stem stitch using three strands of dark grey embroidery thread. Using the same thread, work French knots for the eye centres.

Work the outline of the cheeks in back stitch using three strands of dusky pink embroidery thread.

Work the mouth in back stitch using three strands of crimson embroidery thread.

Work the inner circle around the moon in running stitch, using three strands of bright yellow embroidery thread.

Work the outer circle in running stitch, using three strands of pale pink embroidery thread.

Using fabric glue, attach the braid around the top and bottom of the shade.

Dream a little dream

Most parents agree that their little angels look at their absolute sweetest tucked up in bed. This motif is the perfect adornment for children's bed linen – if only to encourage them to close their eyes and fall asleep. I've used a ready-made cot-size pillowcase with a drawn threadwork border but it would work just as well on a regular-sized pillowcase.

Get stitching ...

First transfer the pattern of the sleeping child on page 112 onto the corner of your pillowcase.

Work the face outline in stem stitch using three strands of dusky pink embroidery thread. Using the same thread, work the nose and hands in back stitch.

Work the cheeks in satin stitch using three strands of pale pink embroidery thread.

Work the hair in stem stitch using three strands of mid-brown embroidery thread.

Work the eyes in back stitch using two strands of dark grey embroidery thread. Using the same thread, work the lashes in straight stitch.

Work the mouth in back stitch using three strands of dark pink emroidery thread.

Work the blanket in blanket stitch using three strands of lime green embroidery thread.

Work the moon in bright yellow back stitch and the stars in deep yellow star stitch.

You will need

✕ Embroidery thread (floss) in the following colours:
Dusky pink for the face, hands and nose
Pale pink for the cheeks
Dark pink for the mouth
Mid-brown for the hair
Bright yellow for the moon
Deep yellow for the stars
Dark grey for the eyes and lashes
Lime green for the blanket

✕ Embroidery needle

✕ Embroidery scissors

✕ Small pillowcase

Stitches used

Straight stitch, star stitch, back stitch, stem stitch, satin stitch, scallop stitch, blanket stitch

stitch it!

This motif is also great on a child's dressing gown, a cosy fleece blanket or a plain woollen cushion on a bedroom chair.

! Please note that pillows are not suitable for children under the age of 12 months because of the risks of overheating and suffocation.

Sleep

Bunny hugs

You will need

- ✗ Embroidery thread (floss) in the following colours:
  Bright pink and mid-blue for the bunny outlines
  Turquoise and deep pink for the dresses and flower petals
  Lime green for the dress stripes and flower centre (blue bunny)
  Leaf green for the dress stripes and **deep yellow** for the flower centre (pink bunny)
  Dark grey for the eyes and noses
- ✗ Embroidery needle
- ✗ Embroidery scissors
- ✗ Small pieces of pale blue and pale pink felt (two of each colour)
- ✗ A small amount of polyester toy stuffing
- ✗ Matching threads for your felt
- ✗ Sewing scissors
- ✗ Standard sewing needle

Stitches used

Straight stitch, running stitch, chain stitch, lazy daisy stitch, French knot

stitch it!

This design is also perfect for a baby's sleep suit or a baby's hat. You could string a group of bunnies together to make a decoration or mobile.

Rabbits are about the cutest animals ever with their fluffy coats and twitchy noses – until, of course, they munch their way through the prized lettuces in your vegetable patch. Thankfully, when these little embroidered creatures have finished playing outside, they're ready to go upstairs to bed.

Get stitching ...

First transfer the bunny patterns from page 113 onto your felt.

Work the outline in chain stitch using three strands of bright pink or mid-blue embroidery thread.

Work the outline of the dresses in chain stitch using three strands of either turquoise or deep pink embroidery thread.

Work the stripes of the dresses in running stitch using three strands of lime or leaf green embroidery thread.

Work the flower petals in lazy daisy stitch using three strands of turquoise or deep pink embroidery thread. Work French knots for the flower centres using three strands of either lime green or deep yellow embroidery thread.

Work French knots for the eyes using four strands of dark grey embroidery thread. Using the same thread, work a simple cross for the nose and mouth.

To make the bunny embroidery into a stuffed creature, place it right side up on a piece of matching felt. Work a row of small running stitches around the edge, leaving an opening down the right-hand side of the dress. Trim close to the edge, taking care not to cut through the stitching. Stuff the bunnies lightly and continue your running stitch to close the gap.

Work

3

Home sweet home

One of my favourite childhood images is of fairies' and elves' toadstool cottages. They seemed so perfect with their tiny windows and front doors and I could imagine all manner of miniature accessories inside. This toadstool cottage embroidered on felt has been used to jazz up a plain address book bought cheaply from a stationery store.

Get stitching ...

First transfer the toadstool pattern from page 114 onto your piece of cream felt.

Work the outline of the toadstool roof in chain stitch using three strands of red embroidery thread. Work the spots in chain stitch using three strands of pale blue embroidery thread.

Work the sides of the toadstool in stem stitch using three strands of pale brown embroidery thread.

Work the window in back stitch using three strands of turquoise embroidery thread.

Work the outline of the door in chain stitch using two strands of orange embroidery thread. Work the door planks in running stitch using the same thread. Work a French knot for the doorknob using three strands of dark grey embroidery thread.

Work the flowers in lazy daisy stitch using three strands of bright pink embroidery thread. Work French knots for the centres using three strands of bright yellow embroidery thread, remembering to wind your thread just once round the needle instead of the normal twice.

Work the flower stems in back stitch using two strands of leaf green embroidery thread. Using the same thread work lazy daisy stitches for the leaves.

You will need

✕ Embroidery thread (floss) in the following colours:
Red for the toadstool top and border of the book's spine
Pale blue for the spots
Pale brown for the toadstool stalk
Turquoise for the window
Orange for the door
Dark grey for the door knob
Bright pink for the flowers
Bright yellow for the flower centres
Leaf green for the flower stems and leaves
Lime green for the grass
Cream for the borders

✕ Embroidery needle

✕ Embroidery scissors

✕ A piece of cream felt measuring 10 x 12 cm (4 x 4¾ in), rounded at the corners

✕ Two 23 cm (9 in) squares of lime green felt

✕ A piece of grey felt for the spine

✕ An A5 size hardback address book (approx 15 x 21 cm/ 6 x 8¼ in)

✕ Fabric glue

✕ Sewing scissors

Stitches used

Straight stitch, running stitch, back stitch, stem stitch, chain stitch, lazy daisy stitch, blanket stitch, French knot

Work the grass in lime green straight stitch.

Trim the lime green felt squares so they are just slightly larger than the cover of your book. The grey felt for the spine should be the same length as the lime green squares and about 5 cm (2 in) wide.

Work a row of running stitches around the top and outer edge of both pieces of lime green felt using three strands of cream embroidery thread. Work a row of running stitches down both sides of the grey felt spine using three strands of red embroidery thread.

Fasten the toadstool embroidery to one of the pieces of lime green felt with blanket stitch, using three strands of cream embroidery thread.

Using fabric glue, stick the covers and spine in place on the notebook.

stitch it!

This motif is also great as a framed picture for a young child's bedroom, on a greeting card for someone moving home or on a simple calico shoe bag.

Pen friends

Lots of people are fed up with emails these days and I'm predicting that old-fashioned letter-writing will stage a comeback. So here's an embroidered pen for you to stamp your mark on your pencil case – and other items too, of course. I made this simple pencil case from two small pieces of faded denim and a zip, but you could just as easily use a plain ready-made fabric pencil case.

Get stitching ...

First transfer the pen pattern on page 114 onto the pencil case or the fabric that you are using.

Work the pen outline in stem stitch using three strands of deep pink embroidery thread. Using the same thread, add two straight stitches at the base of the barrel, then, using six strands of the same thread, work the clip in chain stitch.

Work the grip section of the pen in stem stitch using three strands of lime green embroidery thread.

Work the nib in back stitch using three strands of black embroidery thread. Add a straight stitch and French knot at the centre.

Work the squiggle in running stitch using three strands of turquoise embroidery thread.

stitch it!

This motif is also suitable for a bookmark, a fabric school bag or a felt wall pocket.

Wise old owl

Owls have always been considered clever birds, which makes this wise old bird the ideal decoration for your book bag. You could sew the owl onto a ready-made calico bag but if you want something a little different, like the bag shown here, see page 105 for some simple instructions. If you are making you own bag, embroider the front piece of the bag before you seam the bag together.

Get stitching ...

First transfer the owl pattern on page 115 onto your bag or fabric.

Outline the body in chain stitch using three strands of crimson embroidery thread.

Work the outline of the top of the head and wings in chain stitch using three strands of mauve embroidery thread.

Work the outer eyes in chain stitch using three strands of leaf green embroidery thread. Make a French knot for the centre of the eyes using three strands of dark brown embroidery thread. Using the same thread, make a ring of small straight stitches on the inside of the outer eyes.

Outline the breast in chain stitch using three strands of pale orange embroidery thread. Work the lines across the breast in running stitch using three strands of lime green embroidery thread.

Work the beak in satin stitch using three strands of bright orange embroidery thread, adding a couple of back stitches along the sides of the beak.

Work the branch in stem stitch using three strands of mid-brown embroidery thread.

Make the legs and claws in stem stitch using three strands of pale orange embroidery thread.

Work the outline of the leaves in stem stitch using three strands of mid-green embroidery thread. Using the same thread, work the centre vein of the leaves in running stitch.

If you are making your own bag, now sew the bag pieces together.

You will need

✕ Embroidery thread (floss) in the following colours:
Crimson for the body outline
Mauve for the top of the head and wings
Leaf green for the outer eyes
Dark brown for the eye centres and small eye lines
Pale orange for the breast outline, legs and claws
Lime green for the lines across the breast
Bright orange for the beak
Mid-green for the leaves
Mid-brown for the branch

✕ Embroidery needle

✕ Embroidery scissors

✕ A ready-made cotton bag or, if you want to make your own bag, fabrics, matching threads, a sewing machine, sewing scissors and an iron

Stitches used

Straight stitch, running stitch, back stitch, stem stitch, satin stitch, chain stitch, French knot

stitch it!

This design looks great as a picture for your study wall, on a fleece throw for a playroom or den or made into a small felt or calico toy.

Ring my bell

You will need

- ✕ Embroidery thread (floss) in the following colours:
  Red for the outline of the phone and receiver
  Dark grey for the dial and flex
  Bright yellow for the finger holes on the dial
- ✕ Embroidery needle
- ✕ Embroidery scissors
- ✕ A 23-cm (9-in) square of green felt
- ✕ Matching thread for the felt
- ✕ A snap fastener
- ✕ A contrasting button
- ✕ Standard sewing needle or sewing machine
- ✕ Sewing scissors

Stitches used

Running stitch, back stitch, stem stitch, French knot

stitch it!

This design looks great on the cover of a small book where you keep your phone numbers, on a fabric doorstop for your study or office or on a felt wall pocket.

Even those who remain sceptical about the benefits of modern technology agree that mobile phones have become one of life's essentials. If, like me, you can never find the sleek black phone lurking at the bottom of your handbag, it's time to make it a bright new home.

Get stitching …

⊙ Using your phone as a guide, cut two pieces of felt to make your phone case, plus two pieces approximately 6 x 3 cm (2½ x 1¼ in) for a fastening strap at the top.

⊙ Transfer the phone pattern on page 115 onto one of the felt pieces.

⊙ Work the receiver and majority of the outline of the phone in stem stitch using three strands of red embroidery thread. Work the two prongs at the top of the phone in back stitch, using the same thread. Work the horizontal line below the dial in back stitch, again using the same thread.

⊙ Outline the dial in back stitch using three strands of dark grey embroidery thread. Work a French knot at the centre of the dial using the same thread. Make French knots to represent the holes in the dial using three strands of bright yellow embroidery thread.

⊙ Work the flex in running stitch using three strands of dark grey embroidery thread.

⊙ Using running sitch, sew the front and back pieces of the phone case together by hand or with a machine and run a line of stitching round the top.

⊙ Fasten the two strap pieces together in the same way and fasten the strap to the inside of the back of the case. Sew the button to the front of the strap and add a snap fastener under the button and in a corresponding place on the front of the case.

Relax

4

The perfect pooch

Do you love the idea of owning a dog but are you put off by the commitment and the worry of inclement weather? This embroidered picture will help you enjoy some of benefits of dog ownership without the hassle. The picture is embroidered on cream felt and displayed in a hand-painted and distressed frame.

Get stitching ...

First transfer the walking the dog pattern on page 117 onto your piece of felt.

Outline the man's face in stem stitch using two strands of flesh pink embroidery thread. Using the same thread, work the hands in scallop stitch and a small straight stitch for the nose.

Work the hair in back stitch using three strands of ginger brown embroidery thread.

Work the mouth in back stitch using three strands of deep pink embroidery thread.

Make two French knots for the man's eyes using three strands of dark grey embroidery thread.

Work the jumper in stem stitch using three strands of red embroidery thread. Work a row of small straight stitches along the lower edge using the same thread.

Work the trousers in stem stitch using three strands of turquoise embroidery thread.

Work the boots in chain stitch using three strands of dark green embroidery thread.

Work the dog's lead in chain stitch using four strands of bright orange embroidery thread.

Outline the dog in chain stitch using three strands of dark grey embroidery thread. Work the dog markings in chain stitch using two strands of pale blue embroidery thread.

You will need

- Embroidery thread (floss) in the following colours:
  Flesh pink for face, nose and hands
  Deep pink for the mouth
  Ginger brown for the hair
  Red for the jumper
  Turquoise for the trousers
  Dark green for the boots
  Bright orange for the dog lead
  Dark grey for the man's eyes and dog
  Pale blue for the dog's markings
  Black for the dog's eye and nose
  Lime green for the grass
  Dusky pink for the flower petals
  Pale orange for the flower centres
  Pale olive green for the flower stems and leaves
  Bright yellow for the sun
- A red crayon for colouring the cheeks
- Embroidery needle
- Embroidery scissors
- A piece of cream felt measuring 25.5 x 20 cm (10 x 8 in)
- A wooden frame to take a picture 25.5 x 20 cm (10 x 8 in)

Stitches used

Straight stitch, back stitch, stem stitch, chain stitch, lazy daisy stitch, scallop stitch, French knot

 Make a French knot for the dog's eye using three strands of black embroidery thread. Make another French knot for the dog's nose using six strands of black embroidery thread.

 Work the flower petals in lazy daisy stitch using three strands of dusky pink embroidery thread. Make French knots for the flower centres using three strands of pale orange embroidery thread.

 Work a series of straight stitches for the grass using three strands of lime green embroidery thread.

 Work the centre of the sun in chain stitch using three strands of bright yellow embroidery thread. Using the same thread, make straight stitches for the rays.

 Use the red crayon to mark the cheeks.

stitch it!

This motif also looks great on a living room cushion, a calico bag or a boy's apron.

The long and short of it

If you're a dog lover, chances are you can't resist a dachshund – the combination of slightly comical looks and lively personality are so appealing. They are also the ideal shape to embroider on anything long and thin! This little canine has been embroidered on a bookmark made from felt scraps.

Get stitching ...

First transfer the dog pattern on page 116 onto the cream felt.

Work the majority of the dog outline in stem stitch using three strands of mid-brown embroidery thread. For the front paw, just showing under the sleeve of the jumper, work in back stitch using the same thread and for the top of the neck work a single straight stitch.

Make the jumper outline in chain stitch using three strands of lime green embroidery thread. Using the same thread, work a row of chain stitch at the bottom of the neck of the jumper. Again using the same thread, work a row of back stitch at the top of the lower rib section of the jumper and a single straight stitch at the top of the rib section of the sleeve. Work a series of single straight stitches to represent the ribbing at the lower, neck and sleeve edges of the jumper.

Work a single straight stitch for the mouth using three strands of red embroidery thread.

Make a French knot for the eye using three strands of dark grey embroidery thread.

Make a French knot for the nose using six strands of dark grey embroidery thread.

Lay the cream felt on the lime green felt. Work a row of running stitches round the cream felt using three strands of red embroidery thread.

stitch it!

This design looks great on a tie for a dog lover, a small picture to hang by the hook for your dog leads or even on a specially made dog's coat.

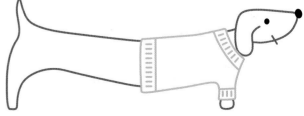

Blooming marvellous

Everyone loves flowers. So when it's chilly outside and the fields and meadows look bare, it's time to embroider your own. This design is shown on a small handmade cushion made from oddments of fabric. It works just as well on a plain ready-made cushion but if you want to make your own, see page 106.

Get stitching ...

First transfer the flowers pattern on page 116 onto your cushion or fabric panel. The width of the fabric panel should be greater than the height.

Work the stalks of the three flowers in stem stitch using three strands of olive green embroidery thread. Using the same thread, work the leaves of the middle flower in stem stitch.

Make the leaves of the outer flowers in stem stitch using three strands of lime green embroidery thread, adding a row of running stitch up the middle of the leaves of the tall flower.

Work the inner circle on the head of the tall flower in chain stitch using three strands of bright pink embroidery thread. Using the same thread, make the petals in lazy daisy stitch. Work the outer circle of the flower in chain stitch using three strands of turquoise embroidery thread.

Work the circle on the head of the middle flower in chain stitch using three strands of royal blue embroidery thread. Make the petals in chain stitch using three strands of mauve embroidery thread.

You will need

- ✕ Embroidery thread (floss) in the following colours:
  Olive green for all three stalks and the leaves of the middle flower
  Lime green for the leaves on the outer two flowers
  Bright pink and turquoise for the tall flower
  Mauve and royal blue for the middle flower
  Deep pink and pale orange for the small flower
- ✕ Embroidery needle
- ✕ Embroidery scissors
- ✕ A plain cushion cover or, if you want to make your own cover, fabrics, matching threads, a snap fastener, a few odd buttons, a sewing machine, sewing scissors, and an iron. The piece of fabric for the embroidery should measure 21 x 22 cm (8¼ x 8¾ in)
- ✕ A small pink and a small yellow button

Stitches used

Running stitch, stem stitch, chain stitch, lazy daisy stitch, French knot

Work the head of the small flower in chain stitch using three strands of deep pink embroidery thread. Make French knots for the stamens using three strands of pale orange embroidery thread.

Sew the buttons in the centre of the tall and middle flowers.

If making your own cover, sew the pieces of the front of the cushion together and add the braid before completing the cover.

stitch it!

This design also looks great as a picture on a bedroom wall, on a bag or on lace-trimmed bed linen.

Knit one, purl one

Knitting is an enduring craze in the world of crafts, so you're bound to know someone who could do with a brand-new box to hold all their projects. I made this simple fabric cover and lining for a shoe box from a piece of cotton drill and some left over curtain fabric. You could just as easily use a ready-made fabric box but if you want to make your own, see page 107.

Get stitching ...

First transfer the knitting pattern on page 117 onto your fabric or fabric box.

Work the ball of wool in back stitch using three strands of deep pink embroidery thread.

Work the knitting needles in stem stitch using three strands of mid-green embroidery thread.

stitch it!

This motif is also suitable for a knitting bag, a craft apron or a felt book cover for a collection of knitting patterns.

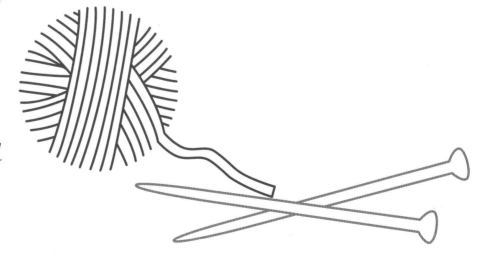

Play

5

Jump for joy

High, low, medium, slow – jolly ol' pepper and away we go! Goodness knows where popular skipping rhymes like this come from but they're a great reminder of how we girls used to spend our time. I made this apron from calico and a simple homemade bias binding trim. You could just as easily use a ready-made apron but if you want to make your own, see page 108.

Get stitching ...

First transfer the skipping girl pattern on page 118 onto the apron or your pocket fabric.

Work the face and legs in stem stitch using two strands of flesh pink embroidery thread. Using the same thread work the arms in stem stitch and the hands in scallop stitch. Again using the same thread, work two straight stitches, one over the other, for the nose.

Make the hair in back stitch using two strands of bright orange embroidery thread.

Work the mouth in back stitch using two strands of red embroidery thread.

Make French knots for the eyes using two strands of dark grey embroidery thread. Make the eyelashes in straight stitch using a single strand of dark grey embroidery thread.

Outline the dress in chain stitch using two strands of lime green embroidery thread. Work the dress collar and pocket in back stitch using the same thread. Again using the same thread, work a line of small running stitches for the dress pocket border.

You will need

✗ Embroidery thread (floss) in the following colours:
Flesh pink for the face, nose, arms, hands and legs
Bright orange for the hair
Lime green for the dress
Red for the shoes and mouth
Mauve for the skipping rope
Bright yellow for the flowers
Mid green for the grass and running stitch border
Dark grey for the eyes

✗ A red crayon for the cheeks

✗ Embroidery needle

✗ Embroidery scissors

✗ A ready-made apron or, if you want to make your own apron, fabrics, matching threads, a sewing machine, sewing scissors and an iron. If you are making your own apron, you will need a piece of fabric for the pocket measuring 20 x 23 cm (8 x 9 in)

Stitches used

Straight stitch, running stitch, back stitch, stem stitch, satin stitch, chain stitch, lazy daisy stitch, scallop stitch, French knot

Work the main part of the shoes in satin stitch using two strands of red embroidery thread. Using the same thread, work a back stitch border around the shoes and a single straight stitch for the bar of the shoes.

Make the skipping rope in running stitch using three strands of mauve embroidery thread and work the rope handles in satin stitch using the same thread.

Work the flowers in lazy daisy stitch using three strands of bright yellow embroidery thread.

Work the grass in straight stitch using three strands of mid-green embroidery thread.

If you are making your own apron, once the pocket has been stitched on the apron, work a running stitch border using three strands of mid-green embroidery thread.

stitch it!

This design also looks great on a cushion for a little girl's room, on a fabric storage box for toys or as a framed picture in the playroom.

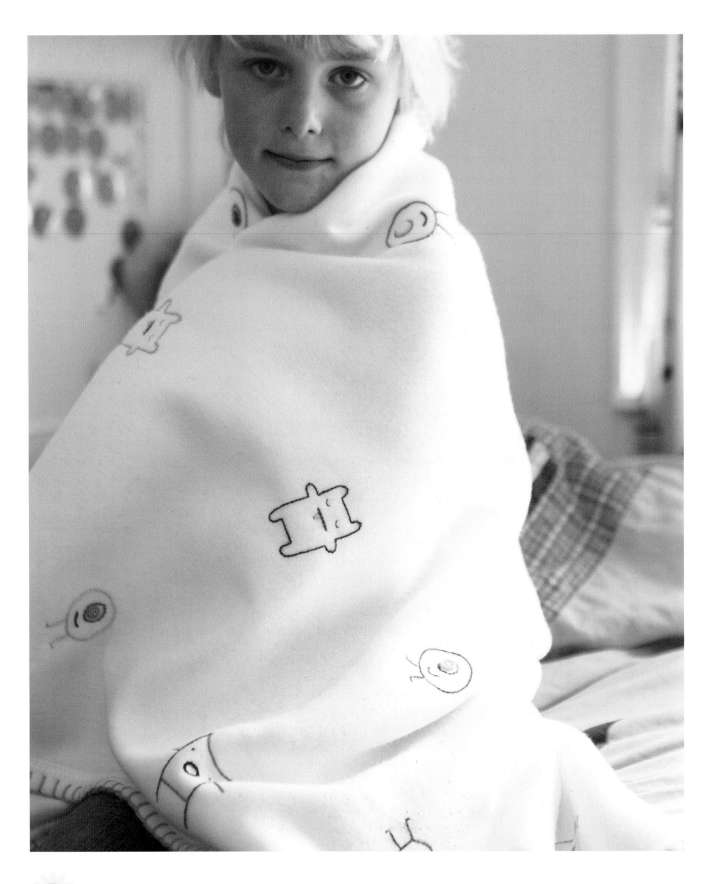

Three beasties

Cute is good, but not all embroidery has to be sugary sweet. So what could be better than an embroidered monster – or three? These monsters have been stitched onto an inexpensive ready-made fleece throw.

the monster patterns on page 118 onto your fabric.

You will need

✗ Embroidery thread (floss) in the following colours:
Bright orange, royal blue, pale blue, turquoise, bright yellow, jade green, emerald, mint green, purple, lilac and lime green for the monsters' bodies
Red, deep and bright pink for the mouths
Mid pink for the tongues
Dark grey for the eyes

✗ A selection of small buttons for the eyes of the round monsters

✗ Embroidery needle

✗ Embroidery scissors

✗ A cream fleece throw (the one shown here measures 170 x 94 cm/67 x 37 in)

✗ Pale olive green double knitting wool for the blanket stitch border

Stitches used

Back stitch, stem stitch, chain stitch, scallop stitch, blanket stitch, French knot

stitch it!

This design is also great on greeting cards and gift tags, on bed linen and on children's T-shirts.

Get stitching ...

First transfer the monster patterns on page 118 onto your fabric. Space them evenly over the throw at different angles to make them look 'scattered' over the fleece.

There are three types of monsters: the round monster; the sleeping monster; the pointy-eared monster.

Outline all the monsters in stem stitch, using three strands of embroidery thread, in a variety of colours (see box left).

For the round monster, work the eye surround in stem stitch using three strands of embroidery thread in the colour of your choice. Work the mouth in chain stitch using three strands of either red, deep or bright pink embroidery thread.

For the sleeping monster, work the eyes in back stitch using three strands of dark grey embroidery thread. Work the mouth in chain stitch using three strands of either red, deep or bright pink embroidery thread. Work a

single scallop stitch for the tongue using three strands of mid-pink embroidery thread.

For the pointy-eared monster, work the mouth in chain stitch using three strands of either red, deep or bright pink embroidery thread. Make a French knot for each eye using three strands of dark grey embroidery thread.

Sew on the buttons for eyes on the round monsters.

Work a blanket stitch border round the entire throw using the double knitting wool.

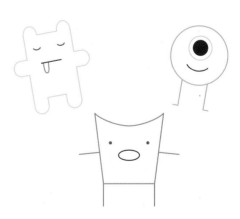

Big wheels keep on turning

Lots of little (and big) boys adore anything to do with cars and trucks, so why not make them some transport wall pockets for all their bits and pieces? The wall pockets are really simple to make.

Get stitching...

First transfer the transport patterns on page 119 onto your pieces of felt. Remember to position your felt so that the height is greater than the width.

Outline the truck cab and base in stem stitch using three strands of royal blue embroidery thread.

Outline the back of the truck in stem stitch using three strands of turquoise embroidery thread. Using the same thread, work the markings in running stitch.

Work the truck window in stem stitch using three strands of mid-grey embroidery thread.

Outline the car in stem stitch using three strands of red embroidery thread.

Work the car windows in stem stitch using three strands of dark grey embroidery thread.

Outline the main part of the caravan in stem stitch using three strands of emerald embroidery thread. Work the tow hook in back stitch using the same thread.

Work the caravan door and window outlines in stem stitch using three strands of bright orange embroidery thread. Work a row of running stitch for the trim using the same thread.

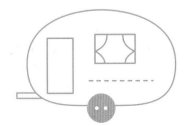

You will need

X **Embroidery thread (floss)** in the following colours:
Red for the car
Dark grey for the car windows
Royal blue for the truck cab and base
Turquoise for the back of the truck
Mid grey for the truck windows
Emerald for the caravan body
Bright orange for the caravan door, window and trim
Mauve for the caravan curtains

X **Two medium green buttons** for the car

X **Two medium red buttons** for the truck

X **One mauve button** for the caravan

X **Embroidery needle**

X **Embroidery scissors**

X **Six pieces of cream felt**, each measuring 16 x 17 cm (6¼ x 6¾ in), two for each pocket

X **Three 15-cm (6-in) lengths of ribbon or tape**, one for each pocket loop

X **Sewing thread** to match your felt

X **Standard sewing needle** or sewing machine

X **Sewing scissors**

Stitches used

Running stitch, back stitch, stem stitch

⊞ Work the curtains in back stitch using three strands of mauve embroidery thread.

⊞ Fasten the red buttons on the truck, the green buttons on the car and the mauve button on the caravan.

⊞ Seam two pieces of felt together to make each pocket, leaving a seam allowance of 1 cm (⅜ in). Turn down 1cm (⅜ in) at the top and stitch in place. Sew a loop of ribbon or tape on the back of each pocket. Hang them on nails, doorknobs and drawer handles.

stitch it!

This motif is also fun on a T-shirt, on a simple calico bag or on a bed cover for a child's room.

Elephants on parade

Who doesn't adore elephants, particularly those floppy, big-footed babies? Inspired by the beautifully decorated elephants that take part in Indian festivals, this cute pair is really simple to make. Once you've embroidered them, just sew around them, turn them and get stuffing. I've made a mother and baby to start, but you could easily whip up a whole herd.

Get stitching ...

First transfer the elephant patterns on page 120 onto your fabric.

For the mother elephant, outline the elephant in chain stitch using three strands of dark grey embroidery thread. Using the same thread, work the ear in running stitch.

For the flower petals, make 6 lazy daisy stitches using six strands of mauve embroidery thread. Make a French knot for the flower centre using six strands of orange embroidery thread.

For the toenails, work three scallop stitches using three strands of dusky pink embroidery thread.

Make a French knot for the centre of the eye using three strands of royal blue embroidery thread. Work seven straight stitches around the eye centre using three strands of leaf green embroidery thread.

For the baby elephant, work exactly as the mother elephant but use pale blue thread for the body and ear, red for the flower petals and yellow for the flower centre.

Trim around both your elephant embroideries leaving a few centimetres (an inch or so) of fabric all the way round.

Place each embroidery face down on a second piece of fabric that is

You will need

- ✕ Embroidery thread (floss) in the following colours:

  For the mother elephant
  Dark grey for the outline and ear
  Mauve for the flower
  Orange for the flower centre
  Royal blue for the centre of the eye
  Leaf green for the outer eye
  Dusky pink for the toenails

  For the baby elephant
  Pale blue for the outline and ear
  Red for the flower
  Yellow for the flower centre
  Royal blue for the centre of the eye
  Leaf green for the outer eye
  Dusky pink for the toenails

- ✕ Embroidery needle
- ✕ Embroidery scissors
- ✕ A small amount of mid-weight woven cotton fabric in off-white
- ✕ Matching sewing thread for your fabric
- ✕ 15 g (½ oz) polyester toy stuffing (this will be sufficient to stuff both elephants)
- ✕ Standard sewing needle or sewing machine
- ✕ Sewing scissors
- ✕ Iron

Stitches used

Straight stitch, running stitch, chain stitch, lazy daisy stitch, scallop stitch, French knot

roughly the same size. Using matching thread, sew around the elephants about 5–7 mm (¼ in) from the edge of the chain stitched outline, leaving a gap between the legs for turning. You can use a sewing machine for this or sew by hand.

⊞ Turn the elephants the right way out through the gap and press

lightly using the iron. To get the seam to lie nicely round the edge of the elephant, try rolling it gently between your dampened thumb and forefinger before you press it.

⊞ Stuff the elephant lightly then sew the gap closed.

stitch it!

This design is perfect on a baby sleepsuit, on a small tote bag or on a cushion for a playroom – you could decorate the cushion with colourful braids or a pom-pom trim.

Dress

6

Dress

A little birdie told me

Note
The main stitch used for this project is chain stitch. This is a very stable stitch and works well on stretchy knitted fabrics such as the cotton of this T-shirt. If you are embroidering this pattern on woven cotton, you could just as easily use stem stitch for the outline of the trunk, branches and treetop, if you prefer.

Sweet little birds used to be a mainstay of embroidery patterns in the 1950s and 1960s. So why did they all disappear? Now, thank goodness, cute has made a comeback – this time with just a hint of contemporary sophistication.

Get stitching ...

• First transfer the bird in a tree pattern on page 122 onto your white T-shirt.

• Outline the tree trunk in chain stitch, using three strands of mid-brown embroidery thread.

• Outline the treetop in chain stitch, using three strands of leaf green embroidery thread.

• Outline each of the apples in chain stitch, using three strands of red embroidery thread.

• Work around the outline of the bird in chain stitch, using two strands of mid-blue embroidery thread and starting at one corner of the tail. Make a couple of straight stitches in the tail before fastening off.

• Make the beak by working two small straight stitches in a 'V' shape, using two strands of yellow embroidery thread.

• Work the eye in tiny back stitches, using a single strand of grey embroidery thread.

• If you like, make a line of running stitch round the hem of the T-shirt, using three strands of red embroidery thread.

stitch it!

This motif also works well on a plain white skirt, on bed linen or on a canvas tote bag.

Blowing in the wind

I love the sight of washing on a line, blowing in the breeze, and the smell of line-dried laundry. You could easily use a ready-made bag for this project, but if you want to make your own, sew together two rectangles of linen, each measuring 36 x 43 cm (14 x 17 in) and embroider the front before you make up the bag.

Get stitching ...

Transfer the washing line pattern on page 121 onto one piece of fabric or onto the front of your bag.

Outline the shirt in stem stitch using three strands of leaf green embroidery thread. Using the same thread, work the collar in back stitch, then work the central line and cuff in running stitch.

Using three strands of red embroidery thread, make French knots for the buttons, winding the thread just once round the needle.

Outline the trousers in stem stitch using three strands of turquoise embroidery thread. Work the hems of the trousers in running stitch using two strands of the same thread.

Outline the dress in stem stitch using three strands of bright pink embroidery thread. Using the same thread, work the pocket in back stitch and the skirt trim in scallop stitch. Work the pocket trim in running stitch using two strands of the same thread.

Make the washing line in running stitch using three strands of dark grey embroidery thread.

Make single straight stitches for the pegs using three strands of terracotta embroidery thread.

Sew on the flowers or work some lazy daisy stitches to make flowers in your chosen colours. If using a ready-made bag, you have now finished.

If you're making your own bag, now stitch the bag together. Seam the two main pieces together at the sides and bottom and double hem the top edge. The drawstring casing is made from a 70 x 3 cm (27½ x 1¼ in) strip of printed cotton. Press down 1.5 cm (¾ in) round all the edges of the strip. Now sew the strip in place about 4 cm (1½ in) down from the top so that the two short edges form a space on the right-hand side for the drawstring, which should be about 1 m (39 in) long. Thread the drawstring through the casing.

stitch it!

Use this design on a cushion, as a simple framed picture for the kitchen or on a clothes peg bag.

Never mind the weather

stitch it!
This design also looks great on trouser pockets, little felt wall pockets or round the border of a tablecloth for an outdoor table.

Plimsolls are comfy and cool for a long, hot summer. And while plain ones have their place, if you want something a little special, try adding your own motifs. It's not half as difficult as it looks – simple, small motifs like these work best.

Get stitching ...

First transfer the weather patterns on page 121 onto the plimsolls.

Outline the cloud in chain stitch using three strands of blue/grey embroidery thread. Work the rain in running stitch using two strands of pale grey embroidery thread.

Outline the sun in chain stitch using three strands of bright yellow embroidery thread. Using the same thread, work a series of straight stitches for the rays.

Work both mouths in back stitch using three strands of crimson embroidery thread.

Make French knots for the eyes of the cloud and sun using three strands of dark grey embroidery thread.

Note

It is fairly easy to embroider plimsolls, particularly if you stuff them with tissue paper. You can secure your thread at the beginning of your work by making a knot in the normal way. However it is a bit harder to secure your thread when you have finished your stitching. Either make a couple of tiny stitches on the front of your work then take your thread to the back and trim, or take your thread to the back of your work and dab it with a spot of fabric glue.

A rose is a rose is a rose

A red rose is shorthand for love and is one of the best-known motifs ever. Although it's been around for so long, I couldn't possibly leave it out of this collection. So here is my very own stitched rose, shown on a ready-made bag.

Get stitching ...

- First transfer the rose pattern on page 122 onto your bag.

- Work the main part of the rose in chain stitch using three strands of deep pink embroidery thread.

- Make French knots for the stamens using three strands of pale orange embroidery thread.

- Work the stalk and leaf outlines in stem stitch using three strands of olive green embroidery thread. Using the same thread, work the veins of the leaves in running stitch.

You will need

- ✗ Embroidery thread (floss) in the following colours:
  Deep pink for the main part of the flower
  Pale orange for the stamens
  Olive green for the stalk and leaves
- ✗ Embroidery needle
- ✗ Embroidery scissors
- ✗ Ready-made fabric bag

Stitches used

Running stitch, stem stitch, chain stitch, French knot

stitch it!

A rose motif looks great on a greeting card for a loved one or on the pocket of your favourite jeans. It also adds a touch of romance to your bed linen.

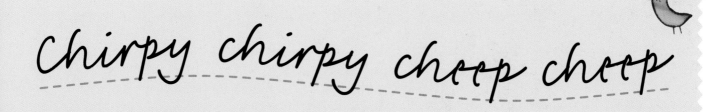

Chirpy chirpy cheep cheep

You will need

- ✗ Embroidery thread (floss) in the following colours:
  Denim blue for the cage
  Bright pink for the bird
  Pale orange for the beak
  Bright orange for the legs
  Dark grey for the eye
  Mauve for the flowers
- ✗ Embroidery needle
- ✗ Embroidery scissors
- ✗ A pair of white jeans

Stitches used

Straight stitch, running stitch, stem stitch, chain stitch, lazy daisy stitch, French knot

stitch it!

This birdie motif is also great on a greeting card, on a felt wall pocket or as a tiny framed picture.

These days we know that birds should really be flying free and not cooped up in a cage – even a pretty Victorian one. So this little fellow, hiding on the pocket of a pair of jeans, is singing to celebrate its freedom!

Get stitching ...

First transfer the birdcage pattern on page 122 onto the pocket of the jeans.

Work the bird in chain stitch using three strands of bright pink embroidery thread.

For the bird's legs work two single straight stitches using three strands of bright orange embroidery thread.

Work two single straight stitches for the beak using six strands of pale orange embroidery thread.

Make a French knot for the eye using three strands of dark grey embroidery thread, remembering to wind the thread just once around the needle instead of the normal twice. Work tiny straight stitches round the eye using a single strand of the same colour thread.

Outline the cage in stem stitch using three strands of denim blue embroidery thread. Using the same thread, work the cage bars and trim along the base of the cage in running stitch. Work the cage loop in chain stitch, again using the same thread.

Make the flowers in lazy daisy stitch using three strands of mauve embroidery thread.

Bath

7

A whale of a time

A whale leaping out of the ocean is a magnificent sight. In all honesty, this whale is unlikely to be doing much leaping but he looks perfect on this ready-made shower cap and would make a jolly addition to many other bathroom items.

Get stitching ...

First transfer the whale pattern on page 124 onto your shower cap.

Outline the whale in chain stitch using three strands of bright blue embroidery thread. Work the mouth in back stitch using three strands of the same thread.

Work the water spout in running stitch using four strands of pale grey embroidery thread.

Make a French knot for the eye using three strands of dark grey embroidery thread. Using the same thread, work small straight stitches round the eye.

stitch it!

This whale looks great on bathroom towels, on a pyjama pocket or on a fabric lampshade for a child's bedroom.

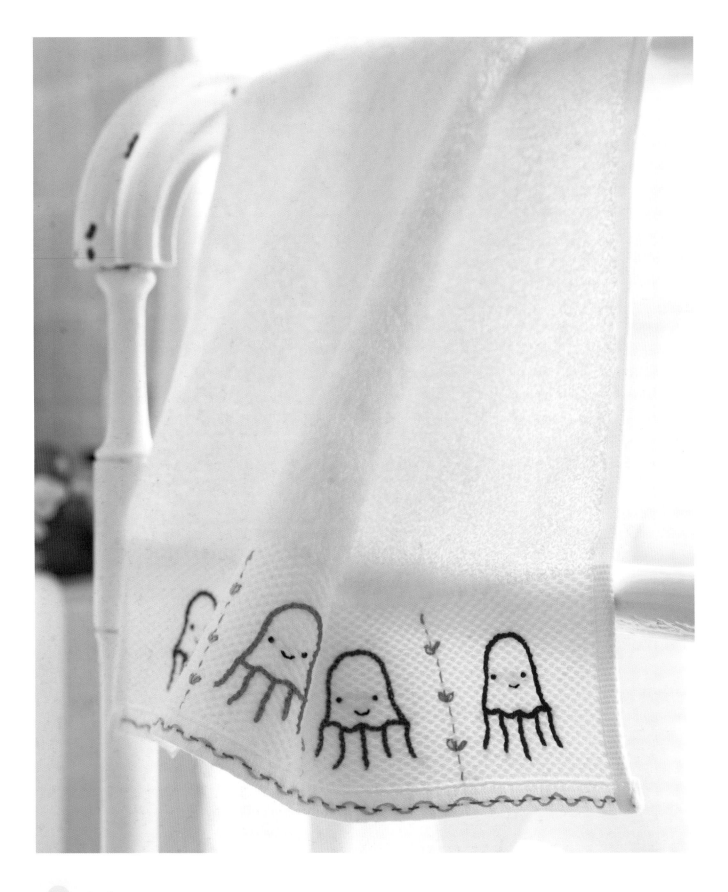

Under the sea

Plain white towels, beloved of hotels everywhere, are... well a bit boring, actually. But who could resist a towel with these delightful little jellyfish? I've stitched these little fellows in shades of pink and red, but you can sew them in any colours you like to match your bathroom.

Get stitching...

First transfer the jellyfish and seaweed pattern on page 124 onto your towel. You will need to make sure your jellyfish and seaweed are evenly spaced across the border of your towel.

Work the body and legs of each jellyfish in chain stitch, using three strands of embroidery thread in either deep pink, bright pink, orange, dusky pink or red.

Work the mouths in back stitch using three strands of purple embroidery thread.

Make French knots for the eyes using three strands of dark grey embroidery thread.

Work a vertical row of running stitch for the seaweed using three strands of leaf green embroidery thread. Work the leaves in lazy daisy stitch.

Make a row of running stitch along the edge of the towel using three strands of mid-blue embroidery thread. Then weave three strands of pale blue embroidery thread through these stitches.

stitch it!

This design looks great on a shower cap, on a bathroom blind or on a cotton bathrobe.

Squeaky clean

Don't you just love that time of day when you can climb into a piping hot bath and soak all your worries away? If you do, then immortalize the moment in a picture stitched on calico, stretched over an inexpensive artist's canvas and stapled in place.

Get stitching ...

First transfer the bath-time pattern on page 123 onto your fabric.

Work the bath and feet in stem stitch using three strands of mauve embroidery thread. Using the same thread, work a couple of small straight stitches on the feet of the bath to represent the claws.

Work the shower and main part of the tap in dark grey stem stitch. Using the same thread, work the handle of the tap in back stitch.

Work the water spray in running stitch using three strands of pale blue embroidery thread. Using the same thread, work the bubbles in back stitch.

Outline the face and arms in stem stitch using three strands of flesh pink embroidery thread. Using the same thread, work the hand in scallop stitch and a single straight stitch for the nose.

Work the mouth in back stitch using three strands of crimson embroidery thread.

Work the hair in back stitch using three strands of terracotta embroidery thread.

Make French knots for the girl's eyes using three strands of dark grey embroidery thread. Work small straight stitches for the eyelashes using two strands of the same thread.

Outline the duck and the wing in chain stitch using two strands of bright yellow embroidery thread. Work two straight stitches for the beak using three strands of bright orange thread.

You will need

× Embroidery thread (floss) in the following colours:
Mauve for the bath
Dark grey for the shower, taps and eyes
Flesh pink for the face, nose and arms
Crimson for the mouth
Pale blue for the water and bubbles
Bright yellow for the duck
Bright orange for the duck's beak
Mint green for the sponge
Bright pink for the curtains
Lime green for the window
Terracotta for the hair
Mid green, leaf green and lime green for the fish

× A red crayon for colouring the cheeks

× Embroidery needle

× Embroidery scissors

× A piece of calico measuring approximately 50 cm (20 in) square

× A 25 x 20 cm (10 x 8 in) square artist's canvas frame

× Sewing scissors

× Iron

× A staple gun and staples

Stitches used

Straight stitch, running stitch, back stitch, stem stitch, chain stitch, scallop stitch, French knot

Work the fish in chain stitch using two strands of each of the three green embroidery threads.

Make a French knot for the fishes' eyes and duck's eye using two strands of dark grey embroidery thread.

Work the sponge in chain stitch using three strands of mint green embroidery thread. Using the same thread, make French knots for the holes.

Make the curtains in stem stitch using three strands of bright pink embroidery thread. Using the same thread, add a row of back stitch at the centre of each curtain and two straight stitches along the hem of each curtain.

Work the top and bottom of the window in stem stitch using three strands of lime green embroidery thread. Make the windowpanes in running stitch using the same thread.

Use the red crayon for the cheeks.

Iron the fabric, then stretch it over the artist's frame and staple in place using the staple gun.

stitch it!

This design is fun on a drawstring bag for storing bath toys, a fabric-covered storage box or on a cushion for a bathroom stool.

Sail away with me

You will need

- ✕ Embroidery thread (floss) in the following colours:
  Denim blue for the sail and stripe on the boat
  Red for the flag and boat
  Mid-grey for the mast and gulls
  Pale blue for the cloud
- ✕ Embroidery needle
- ✕ Embroidery scissors
- ✕ A plain fabric doorstop or, if you want to make your own doorstop, fabric, matching thread, polyester stuffing, rice, a polythene bag, a standard sewing needle, sewing machine, sewing scissors and an iron
- ✕ A length of wide blue ric-rac tape to go around the entire circumference of the doorstop

Stitches used

Running stitch, back stitch, stem stitch, satin stitch, chain stitch

stitch it!

This nautical motif also looks great on a drawstring bag for a boy's bedroom, a greeting card or a T-shirt.

Sailing boats remind me of childhood holidays by the sea. They're cheerful, mysterious and romantic, all at the same time, so it's no wonder that they're such a popular motif in bathrooms around the world. I've used a simple handmade doorstop for the sailing boat here and for instructions on how to make one, see page 109.

Get stitching ...

First transfer the sailing-boat pattern on page 124 onto one of the large surfaces of your doorstop. If you are making your own doorstop, embroider it before you seam it together.

Work the sails in stem stitch using three strands of denim blue embroidery thread.

Work the mast in stem stitch using three strands of mid-grey embroidery thread.

Outline the boat in chain stitch using three strands of red embroidery thread. Make the stripe in running stitch using three strands of denim-blue embroidery thread.

Work the flag in satin stitch using three strands of red embroidery thread. Outline the flag in small back stitches using a single strand of the same thread.

Make the gulls in back stitch, using three strands of mid-grey embroidery thread.

Make the clouds in chain stitch, using three strands of pale blue embroidery thread.

Stitch the blue ric-rac tape around the bottom of the doorstop. If you are making your own doorstop, do this once you have seamed the sides of the doorstop together but before you have stuffed the doorstop or seamed the base.

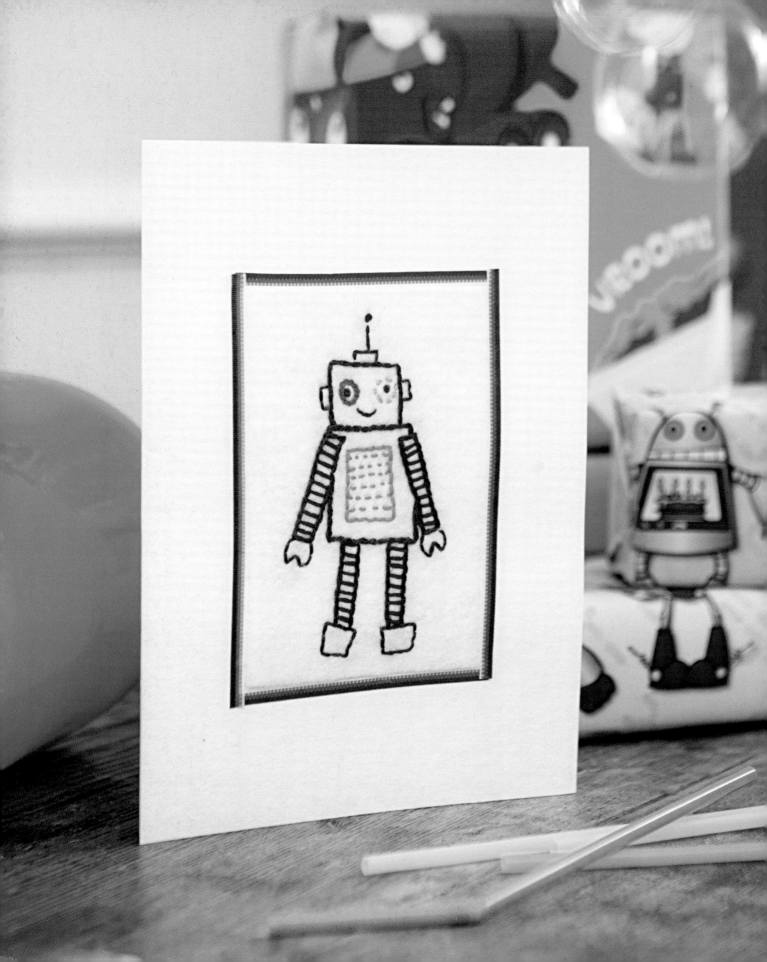

Celebrate

Away with the fairies

Dreamy and mysterious, delicate and floaty – it's no wonder so many little girls (and some bigger ones too) want to look like fairies. If you know anyone who's crazy for the make-believe world of fairies, they'll love this little darling who has been embroidered on felt and stuck on a ready-made card blank.

Get stitching ...

First transfer the fairy pattern on page 125 onto your piece of felt.

Work the face, legs and arms in stem stitch using three strands of light brown embroidery thread. Using the same thread, work the hands in scallop stitch. Work a single straight stitch for the nose, again using the same thread.

Make the hair in back stitch using three strands of dark brown embroidery thread.

Make two French knots for the eyes using three strands of dark grey embroidery thread. Using a single strand of the same thread, make three short straight stitches for the eyelashes.

Work the mouth in back stitch using three strands of red embroidery thread.

Work the outline of the dress in chain stitch using three strands of lime green embroidery thread. Using the same thread, work the base of the bodice in back stitch. Using two strands of the same thread, work the gather lines in running stitch.

Make two French knots for the buttons using three strands of deep pink embroidery thread, winding the thread just once around the needle. Work a row of running stitches across the hem of the dress using two strands of pale pink embroidery thread.

Make the wings in running stitch, using three strands of deep pink embroidery thread.

You will need

✗ Embroidery thread (floss) in the following colours:
Light brown for the face, nose, arms and legs
Dark brown for the hair
Dark grey for the eyes and eyelashes
Red for the mouth
Lime green for the dress
Pale pink for the trim on the dress
Deep pink for the wings, shoes and buttons
Bright yellow for the wand

✗ A pink crayon for the cheeks

✗ Embroidery needle

✗ Embroidery scissors

✗ A piece of white felt measuring 10 x 13 cm (4 x 5¼ in)

✗ A piece of narrow lace for the border measuring approximately 30 cm (12 in)

✗ An A5 size card blank (about 15 x 21 cm/ 6 x 8¼ in)

✗ Fabric glue

Stitches used

Straight stitch, star stitch, running stitch, back stitch, stem stitch, satin stitch, chain stitch, scallop stitch, French knot

Work the shoes in satin stitch using three strands of deep pink embroidery thread. Using the same thread, make a cross at the top of each shoe for the ribbons.

Work the wand in back stitch, using three strands of bright yellow embroidery thread. Using the same thread, add a star stitch at the top to complete the wand.

Colour on the cheeks with the pink crayon.

Using fabric glue, stick the felt panel onto the card blank and stick the narrow lace around the border.

stitch it!

This fairy looks magical on a bag to hold ballet shoes, on a little girl's T-shirt or as a small picture for a bedroom.

cool robot

Robots seem to have been around for ages and are a favourite motif of small boys. Try stitching your own prototype for a boy in your life. This robot has been embroidered on felt and stuck on a ready-made card blank.

You will need

- ✕ Embroidery thread (floss) in the following colours:
  Dark grey for the main outline
  Red for the stripes and antenna
  Turquoise for the central panel
  Purple for the eyes and mouth
  Royal blue for the outline of the left-hand eye
  Lime green for the outline of the right-hand eye
- ✕ Embroidery needle
- ✕ Embroidery scissors
- ✕ A piece of white felt measuring 8 x 12 cm (3¼ x 4¾ in)
- ✕ A piece of narrow self-adhesive ribbon for the border measuring approximately 30 cm (12 in)
- ✕ An A5 size card blank (about 15 x 21 cm/ 6 x 8¼ in)
- ✕ Fabric glue

Stitches used

Straight stitch, running stitch, back stitch, stem stitch, chain stitch, French knot

stitch it!

This design looks great made into a small stuffed toy, on a T-shirt or on some children's placemats.

Get stitching ...

First transfer the robot pattern on page 125 onto your piece of felt.

Outline the head, torso, arms and legs in stem stitch using three strands of dark grey embroidery thread. Using the same thread, work the ears, very top of the head, hands and feet using back stitch.

Work the mouth in back stitch, using three strands of purple embroidery thread. Using the same thread, make two French knots for the centres of the eyes. Work the outer part of the left-hand eye in chain stitch, using two strands of royal blue embroidery thread. Work the outer part of the right-hand eye in running stitch using three strands of lime green embroidery thread.

Make the stripes along the arms and legs in straight stitch using three strands of red embroidery thread. Using the same thread, make the antenna at the top of the head in back stitch with a French knot to represent the antenna tip.

Outline the central panel in back stitch using three strands of turquoise embroidery thread. Using the same thread, work the lines on the panel in running stitch.

Using fabric glue, stick the felt panel on the card blank. Use the narrow self-adhesive ribbon to make a border.

Up the garden path

Snail worship is something of a minority activity and the preserve of the dedicated fan. But who could resist the endearing shelled creature in this picture? If you love wildlife, please try stitching the snail as well as the adorable greenfly-gobbling ladybird! These gift tags are embroidered on scraps of felt that are stuck onto ready-made cardboard luggage labels.

Get stitching ...

First transfer the snail and ladybird patterns on page 126 onto your pieces of felt.

For the snail, work the body in stem stitch using three strands of orange embroidery thread. Using the same thread work the antennae in back stitch with French knots at the end.

Do the shell in stem stitch using three strands of turquoise embroidery thread. Using the same thread, work the coil in running stitch.

Make French knots for the snail's eyes using two strands of dark grey embroidery thread, remembering to wind the thread just once around the needle instead of the normal twice. Using the same thread, work the mouth in back stitch.

Make several single straight stitches for the grass using three strands of lime green embroidery thread.

Make the border in running stitch using three strands of mid-pink embroidery thread.

For the ladybird, work the body in chain stitch using three strands of red embroidery thread. Make French knots for the spots using three strands of black embroidery thread.

Work the face in stem stitch using two strands of dark grey embroidery thread. Using the same thread, make the two antennae in back stitch.

Work the legs in straight stitch using three strands of black embroidery thread.

Make French knots for the eyes using two strands of dark grey embroidery thread. Work the mouth in back stitch using two strands of red embroidery thread.

Do several single straight stitches for the grass using three strands of mid-green embroidery thread.

Work the border in running stitch using three strands of denim blue embroidery thread.

Trim the embroideries and use fabric glue to stick them to the luggage labels.

stitch it!

These cute little creatures also look great on baby clothes, as a border on a curtain or on bunting for a garden room or summer house.

Celebrate

Love is like a butterfly

Nothing reminds me more of summer than watching a butterfly flitting from flower to flower. Sadly, these experiences can't last forever so I whipped up some summery butterfly bunting to keep the memories alive. The butterflies are embroidered on felt pennants, then sewn together on a strip of bias binding.

stitch it!

A butterfly motif is fun on children's clothes, felt wall pockets for a girl's bedroom or as little stuffed creatures strung together to form a mobile.

Get stitching ...

Cut the felt squares into eight triangles or pennants, each measuring 15 cm (6 in) across the base and 18 cm (7 in) from the mid-point of the base to the tip. It is a good idea to make a pattern from cardboard, which you can then simply draw around.

Now transfer the butterfly pattern on page 126 onto your pennants, so that each butterfly is situated in the same place on the triangle.

Work the bodies and antennae in stem stitch using three strands of dark grey embroidery thread. Make French knots for the eyes using the same thread, remembering to wind the thread just once round the needle instead of the normal twice. Work the mouth in back stitch, again using the same thread.

Make the wings in chain stitch, using three strands of one of the different brightly coloured threads for each butterfly.

Sew buttons to the top part of the wings for each of the butterflies, using contrasting coloured thread.

Fold the bias binding in half and baste the pennants evenly along the length of the binding, leaving a decent 'tail' at either end to fasten the bunting. Machine or hand-stitch along the edges of the binding, including the 'tails'.

Make your own stuff to stitch

The following are basic instructions on how to make some of the items featured in this book. While a sewing machine is not absolutely essential, your work will be stronger and have a more professional finish if you use one.

All seam allowances are 1 cm (⅜ in). All measurements are given in metric then in imperial figures. To make life easy for yourself, stick to one set of measurements or the other; don't mix the two or the end result may be less than satisfactory!

Table mat

See page 22 and use the photo as a guide.

The finished mat is approximately 22 x 29 cm (or 9 x 12½ in).

Once you have embroidered the main panel of the mat, seam the two short fabric strips to the short sides of the mat and press the seams open. Then sew the two long strips across the top and bottom and press the seams open.

Iron the interfacing onto the backing fabric. Lay the front and back of the mat right sides together and seam around the edge leaving a gap at the middle of the lower edge for turning.

Clip the corners, turn the mat the right way out and press. Top stitch around the outside of the mat about 5 mm (¼ in) from the outside edge.

Cotton bag

You will need

You will need

✕ Two rectangles of cotton fabric, each measuring about 32 cm (12½ in) square

✕ Contrasting fabric to make the binding

See page 49 and use the photo as a guide.

The finished bag (excluding handles) is approximately 25 cm (10 in) square.

● For the binding, cut some 6-cm (2½-in) wide strips of fabric on the bias. You will need two 21-cm (8¼-in) long strips for the bag top and two 56-cm (22-in) long strips for the sides and handles. Seam strips together diagonally if you do not have sufficient fabric to cut single lengths.

● Follow the diagram below to make your bag template, then cut out two identical pieces of fabric for the front and back of the bag.

● Once you have embroidered the bag front, sew the darts at the bottom of the two bag pieces.

● To prepare the binding, fold the long raw edges of the strips to the centre and press. Then fold the strips in half and press again. Baste the short strips across the tops of the bag pieces and stitch them in place. Then baste and stitch the long pieces in place to form the sides and handles. Now seam the front and back of the bag together and neaten the seams.

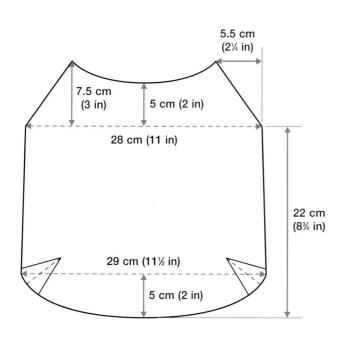

5.5 cm (2¼ in)

7.5 cm (3 in)

5 cm (2 in)

28 cm (11 in)

22 cm (8¾ in)

29 cm (11½ in)

5 cm (2 in)

Cushion cover

See page 59 and use the photo as a guide.

The cushion cover is to fit a 30 cm (12 in) square cushion. The cover is slightly smaller so that the cushion looks plump.

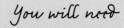 After embroidering the panel, seam it to the side panel and press the seams open. Then seam these pieces to the lower panel and press the seams open. Stitch the braid in place.

For the back of the cushion, hem along one of the long sides of the two back pieces. Seam them to the front of the cushion cover so that the hemmed side of the top back piece overlaps the lower back piece. Clip the corners and turn the right way out.

Stitch the snap fastener at the centre of the overlapped pieces and sew the button in the centre of the lower edge of the top flap, over the snap fastener.

Fabric-lined knitting box

See page 60 and use the photo as a guide.

These details explain how to make a fabric cover for a box such as a large shoebox.

⊞ Loosely measure the base and sides of your box and cut out a shape from your outer fabric and lining fabric, as shown below.

⊞ Sew the four side seams of the outer cover and lining to form two box shapes. Double-hem round the top of the lining fabric (you do not have to hem the fabric for the outer part of the box).

⊞ Once you have embroidered the outer cover, place it over the box and tuck the top down. Then position the lining and pull the top part of the lining over the edges of the box. You may find it useful to position the cover on the box before you start your embroidery in order to work out where to place the motif.

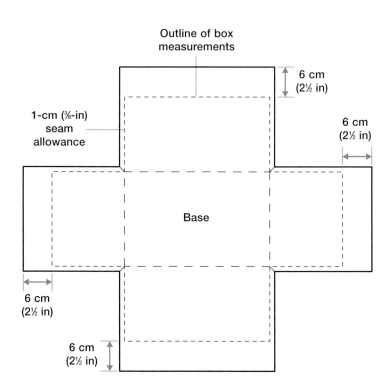

Outline of box measurements

6 cm (2½ in)

6 cm (2½ in)

1-cm (⅜-in) seam allowance

Base

6 cm (2½ in)

6 cm (2½ in)

Child's apron

See page 65 and use the photo as a guide.

The apron will fit a child of approximately 6–10 years old.

For the binding, the ties and trim, cut some 4.5 cm (1¾ in) wide strips of fabric on the bias. You will need a strip measuring 1.7 m (1.9 yd) in length for the waist ties, upper sides and head loop and a strip measuring 1.1 m (1.2 yd) in length for lower sides and hem. Seam strips together diagonally if you do not have sufficient fabric to cut single lengths.

Cut the main piece for the apron using the guidelines below.

Once you have embroidered and stitched the pocket, prepare the binding. Fold the long raw edges of the strips to the centre and press. Then fold the strips in half and press again.

Baste and stitch the binding around the lower sides and bottom first, then baste and stitch the binding round the sides and top, allowing 35 cm (14 in) of binding to form the head loop. Stitch the binding together without the apron fabric to form the waist ties.

You will need

✕ A piece of fabric for the main part of the apron measuring 65 x 48 cm (25½ x 19 in)

✕ A piece of fabric for the pocket measuring 20 x 23 cm (8 x 9 in)

✕ Fabric to make the binding, ties and trim

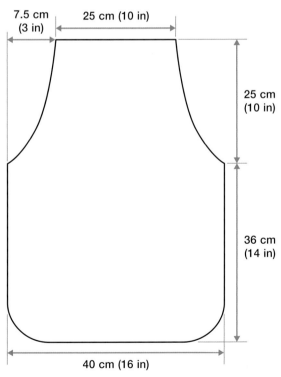

7.5 cm (3 in)

25 cm (10 in)

25 cm (10 in)

36 cm (14 in)

40 cm (16 in)

Doorstop

See page 92 and use the photo as a guide.

You will need

- ✕ A piece of drill fabric or similar measuring 55 x 65 cm (21½ x 25½ in)
- ✕ Enough rice or a mixture of rice and polyester stuffing to fill (you may want to enclose the rice in a polythene bag to protect it from getting damp)

◉ Cut out the doorstop and handle shapes as shown below.

◉ Make the handle of the doorstop by folding up 1 cm (⅜ in) on the long lower edge and 3 cm (1¼ in) at the top edge of the fabric, then fold along the central line and top stitch along both sides.

◉ Fasten the handle to the centre top of the doorstop using 2.5-cm (1-in) stitched squares with a diagonal cross.

◉ Once you have embroidered the doorstop, seam it into a brick shape, leaving a gap on one of the lower edges so that you can stuff it. Stuff the doorstop then stitch the opening closed.

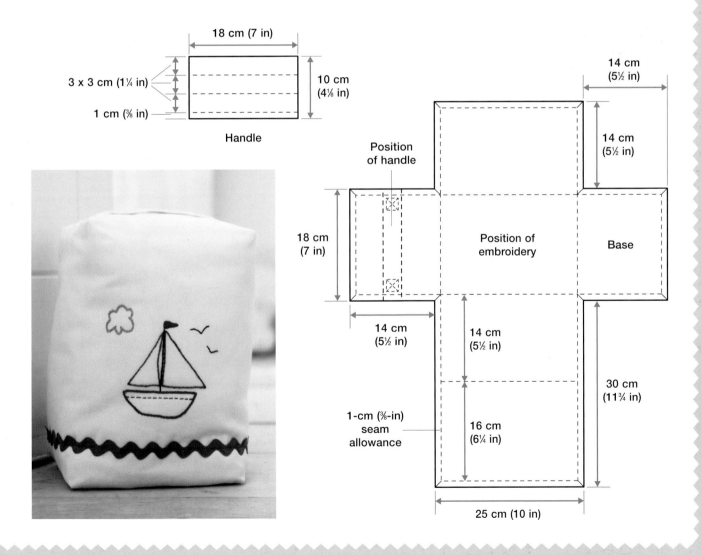

18 cm (7 in)

3 x 3 cm (1¼ in)

1 cm (⅜ in)

10 cm (4⅛ in)

Handle

14 cm (5½ in)

14 cm (5½ in)

Position of handle

18 cm (7 in)

Position of embroidery

Base

14 cm (5½ in)

14 cm (5½ in)

1-cm (⅜-in) seam allowance

16 cm (6¼ in)

30 cm (11¾ in)

25 cm (10 in)

The patterns

Café society
pages 20–21

A nice cup of tea
pages 22–23

Let them eat cake
pages 24–25

Kitchen sink drama
pages 26–27

Sweetest little baby face
pages 28–29

Dream a little dream
pages 38–39

Do the funky chicken
pages 30–31

Give me the moonlight
pages 36–37

The cat's whiskers
pages 34–35

Bunny hugs
pages 40–41

Home sweet home
pages 44–45

Pen friends
pages 46–47

Wise old owl
pages 48–49

Ring my bell
pages 50–51

Blooming marvellous
pages 58–59

The long and short of it
pages 56–57

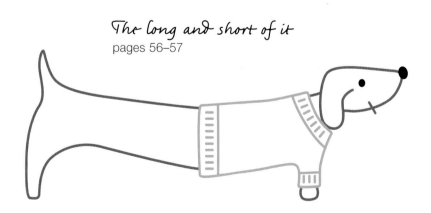

The perfect pooch
pages 54–55

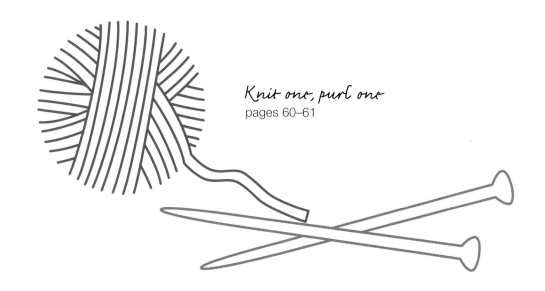

Knit one, purl one
pages 60–61

The patterns   117

Three beasties
pages 66–67

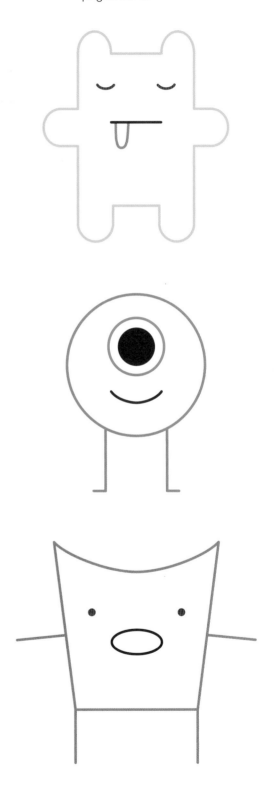

Jump for joy
pages 64–65

Big wheels keep on turning
pages 68–69

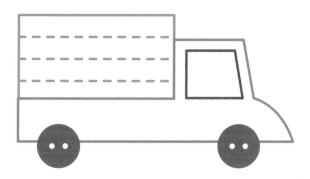

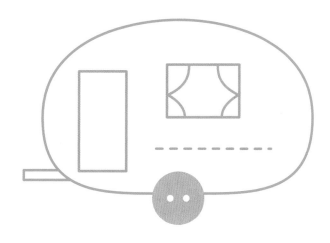

Blowing in the wind
pages 76–77

Never mind the weather
pages 78–79

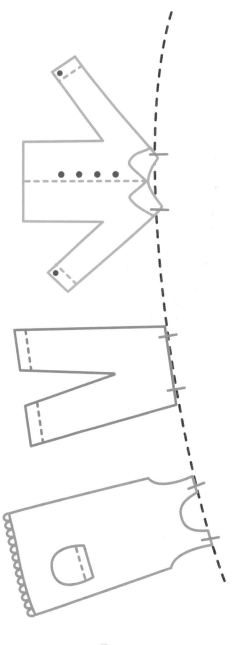

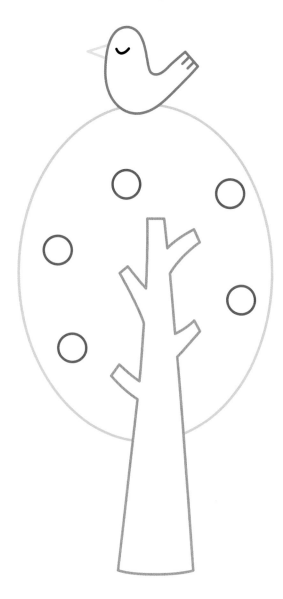

A little birdie told me
pages 74–75

A rose is a rose is a rose
pages 80–81

Chirpy chirpy cheep cheep
pages 82–83

Squeaky clean
pages 90–91

Under the sea
pages 88–89

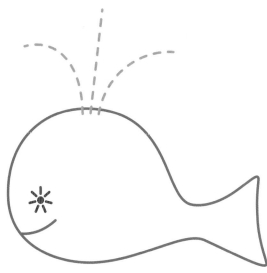

A whale of a time
pages 86–87

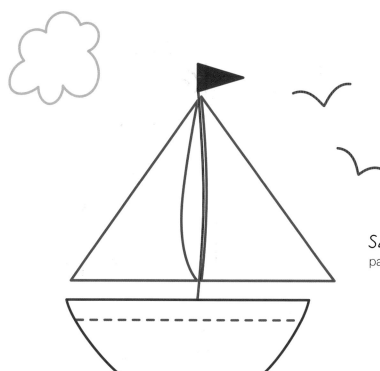

Sail away with me
pages 92–93

Away with the fairies
pages 96–97

Cool robot
pages 98–99

Up the garden path
pages 100–101

Love is like a butterfly
pages 102–103

Index

AB

address books 44–5
aprons
    Café Society 20–1
    Jump for Joy 64–6
Away with the Fairies 96–7
back stitch 13
bags
    Blowing in the Wind 76–7
    A Rose is a Rose is a Rose 80–1
    Wise Old Owl 48–9
bibs 28–9
Big Wheels keep on Turning 68–9
blanket stitch 15
Blooming Marvellous 58–9
Blowing in the Wind 76–7
bookmarks 56–7
books, address 44–5
boxes 60–1
Bunny Hugs 40–1
bunting 102–3

CD

Café Society 20–1
carbon paper 8, 17
cards
    Away with the Fairies 96–7
    Cool Robot 98–9
The Cat's Whiskers 34–5
chain stitch 14
Chirpy Chirpy Cheep Cheep 82–3
Cool Robot 98–9
cup cosies 30–1
cushions 58–9
Do the Funky Chicken 30–1
doorstops 92–3
Dream a Little Dream 38–9

EFG

Elephants on Parade 70–1
embroidery hoops 10
equipment 8–10
fabrics 8, 10
French knots 16
gift tags 100–1
Give Me the Moonlight 36–7

HIJ

Home Sweet Home 44–5
hoops, embroidery 10
irons 10
jeans 82–3
Jump for Joy 64–6

KLM

Kitchen Sink Drama 26–7
Knit One, Purl One 60–1
lampshades 36–7
laundry bags 76–7
lazy daisy stitch 14
Let Them Eat Cake 24–5
A Little Birdie Told Me 74–5
The Long and Short of It 56–7
Love is Like a Butterfly 102–3
measurements 17
mobile phone cases 50–1

NOP

napkins 24–5
needles 8, 10
Never Mind the Weather 78–9
A Nice Cup of Tea 22–4
patterns, transferring 8–9, 17
Pen Friends 46–7
pencil cases 46–7
pens, transferring patterns 8–9, 17
The Perfect Pooch 54–5
phone cases 50–1
pictures
    The Perfect Pooch 54–5
    Squeaky Clean 90–1
pillowcases 38–9
pins 10
plimsolls 78–9
pyjamas 34–5

QRS

Ring My Bell 50–1
A Rose is a Rose is a Rose 80–1
running stitch 12
Sail Away with Me 92–3
satin stitch 14
scallop stitch 15
scissors 9, 10
sewing machines 10
shower caps 86–7
Squeaky Clean 90–1
stabilizer fabrics 10
star stitch 12
stem stitch 13
stitches 11–16
straight stitch 11
Sweetest Little Baby Face 28–9

TU

T-shirts 74–5
tablemats 22–4
tangled thread 16
tea towels 26–7
thimbles 10
thread (floss) 8
    starting and finishing work 11
    tangles and knots 16
threaded running stitch 12
Three Beasties 66–7
throws 66–7
towels 88–9
toys
    Bunny Hugs 40–1
    Elephants on Parade 70–1
transferring patterns 8–9, 17
trimmings 9
Under the Sea 88–9
Up the Garden Path 100–1

VW

wall pockets 68–9
A Whale of a Time 86–7
Wise Old Owl 48–9

The projects in this book have been
sewn using DMC embroidery
threads **www.dmc.com**

With thanks to Paddy and David
Goble and Roger and Louis
Dromard for their enthusiasm
and patience.